Giuseppe Visicato

# The Bureaucracy of Šuruppak

## Administrative Centres, Central Offices, Intermediate Structures and Hierarchies in the Economic Documentation of Fara

Abhandlungen zur Literatur
Alt-Syrien-Palästinas und Mesopotamiens

Band 10

herausgegeben von

Manfried Dietrich — Oswald Loretz

1995
Ugarit-Verlag
Münster

# The Bureaucracy of Šuruppak

## Administrative Centres, Central Offices, Intermediate Structures and Hierarchies in the Economic Documentation of Fara

Giuseppe Visicato

1995
Ugarit-Verlag
Münster

Herstellung: Weihert-Druck GmbH, Darmstadt
Printed in Germany
ISBN 3-927120-35-9
ISSN 0948-3144

Printed on acid-free paper

# TABLE OF CONTENTS

## PREFACE

In the edition of the first volume of the texts of Fara, *Early Dynastic Administrative Tablets of Šuruppak* by F.Pomponio and G.Visicato (IOUN, Series Maior VI, Napoli 1994), the administrative structures which governed the city of Šuruppak between the end of ED II and the beginning of ED III were outlined. From the archeological point of view, this city was one of the most important urban centres in the Early Dynastic period in Babylonia and its role has never been sufficiently clarified. The limits imposed by an edition of the texts did not consent a detailed analysis of the organizational system of Fara.

This volume stems from the need for such an analysis; this is possible only by a thorough examination of the entire administrative documentation of Fara. In particular, the elaboration and analysis of the texts concerning the recruitment of personnel presented in the first two chapters has enabled us, on the one hand, to give an outline of the overall structure of the administration of the city and on the other hand, it has permitted us to clarify the political and economic role of what was described in the previous volume as the "Hexapolis of Šuruppak" at about the middle of the III millenium. In fact, new elements have emerged which point to the existence of a centralized and complex administrative structure and which suggest the presence of an organizational system which seems to be closely linked, at least in some sectors of economic activity, with several cities of central and southern Babylonia. The results reached by us seem to give relevant indications, at least in our opinion, on this historic transition phase of Mesopotamia. The violent destruction of Šuruppak as a consequence of a war, some of whose phases are documented in the texts presented here, marks the beginning of a turbulent period featuring the transitory hegemony of city states; this lasted almost two centuries and concluded that cultural process begun in the Early Dynastic period, but probably already in operation since the Jemdet Nasr period, with the extension of the phenomenon of urbanization to the whole of Babylonia.

The numeration of the texts analysed here follows that of *Šuruppak*. For the texts of CT 50, use was made of the photographs received from the British Museum; for other documents we availed of the collations of Professors Robert Biggs and Aage Westenholz which Professor Francesco Pomponio kindly placed at my disposal.

I would like to thank Professors Manfried L.G.Dietrich and Oswald Loretz for having included this study among the ALASPM series.

I would like to thank in particular Professor Piotr Steinkeller for having read the manuscript and for his many useful suggestions. I wish to thank Professor Francesco Pomponio for his useful advise and incisive criticism. Needless to say, the responsability for the views herein expressed rests enterely with me.

I would like to thank Professor Giovanni Pettinato and the *Unione Accademica Nazionale-Sezione Dizionari Assiri*, for the financial assistance granted to me during the early stages of my research on the administrative documentation of Fara.

Finally, I would like to thank Mr Aiden Feerick for the translation of this volume.

Rome, December 1994

## ABBREVIATIONS

The abbreviations used are those of The Assyrian Dictionary of The Oriental Institute of the University of Chicago, vol. Š, with the following additions.

| | |
|---|---|
| *Akkad* | M.Liverani ed., *Akkad. The First World Empire*, HANE V, Padova 1993 |
| ASJ | *Acta Sumerologica* (Hiroshima) |
| AWL | J.Bauer, *Altsumerische Wirtschaftstexte aus Lagasch*, Studia Pohl 9, Rome 1972 |
| BAOM | *Bulletin of the Ancient Orient Museum* (Tokyo) |
| BSA | *Bulletin of Sumerian Agriculture* (Cambridge U.K.) |
| DAS | M.Lafonte, *Documents administratifs sumériens provenant du site de Tello et conservés au Musée du Louvre*, Paris 1985 |
| D.O.G. | The Deutsche Orient-Gasellschaft |
| Englund, *Fisherei* | R.Englund, *Organisation und Verwaltung der Ur III Fisherei*, BBVO 10, Berlin 1990 |
| ELTS | I.J.Gelb-P.Steinkeller-R.M.Whiting, *Earliest Land Tenure Systems in the Near East: Ancient Kudurrus*, OIP 104, Chicago 1992 |
| FAOS | Freiburger Altorientalische Studien, Stuttgart 1975-- |
| Foster, USP | R.B.Foster, *Umma in the Sargonic Period*, Hamden 1982 |
| *Frühe Schrift* | H.Nissen-P.Damerow-R.K.Englund, *Frühe Schrift und Techniken der Wirtschaftsverwaltung im alten Vorderen Orient*, Berlin 1990 |

| | |
|---|---|
| *Labor* | M.A.Powell ed., *Labor in the Ancient Near East*, AOS 68, New Haven 1987 |
| LAK | A.Deimel, *Die Inschriften von Fara I. Liste der archaischen Keilschriftzeichen,* WVDOG 40, Leipzig 1922 |
| Liverani, *Oriente* | M.Liverani, *Antico Oriente. Storia Società Economia*, Bari 1988 |
| Martin, *Fara* | H.P.Martin, *Fara: A Reconstruction of the Ancient Mesopotamian· City of Shuruppak*, Birmingham 1988 |
| NATN | D.I.Owen, *Neosumerian Archival Texts Primarily from Nippur*, Winona Lake 1982 |
| MVN | Materiali Per Il Vocabolario Neosumerico, Roma 1974-- |
| Nissen, *Protostoria* | H.Nissen, *Protostoria del Vicino Oriente*, Bari 1990 (Italian Translation. of *Grundzüge einer Geschichte der Frühzeit des Vorderen Orients*, Darmstadt 1983) |
| NSRJ | J:Krecher, *Neue sumerische Rechtsur-kunden der 3.Jahrtausends*, ZA 63 (1974), p.145-271 |
| NTSŠ | R.Jestin, *Nouvelles tablettes sumériennes de Šuruppak au Musée d'Istanbul*, Paris 1957 |
| OSP | Old Sumerian and Old Akkadian Texts in Philadelphia chiefly from Nippur, Malibu 1975-- |
| Pomponio, *Prosopografia* | F.Pomponio, *La prosopografia dei testi presargonici di Fara*, Roma 1987 |
| RGTG I | D.O.Edzard-G.Farber-E.Sollberger, *Répertoire Géographique des textes Cunéiformes I*, Weisbaden 1977-- |
| SAT 1 | M.Sigrist, *Texts from the British Museum*, Bethesda 1993 |

| | |
|---|---|
| SD | The Sumerian Dictionary of the University Museum of the University of Pennsylvania, Philadelphia 1984-- |
| Selz, AWAS | G.Selz, *Altsumerische Wirtschaftsurkunden aus Amerikanischen Sammlungen*, FAOS 15, 2, Stuttgart 1993 |
| SNATBM | T.Gomi, *Selected Neo-Sumerian Administrative Texts from the British Museum*, Abiko 1990 |
| SRJ | D.O.Edzard, *Sumerische Rechtsurkunden des III. Jahrtausends aud der Zeit vor der III. Dynastie von Ur*, München 1968 |
| Sigrist, SUL | M.Sigrist, *Textes Économiques Néo-Sumériens de L'Université de Syracuse*, Paris 1983 |
| *Šuruppak* | F.Pomponio-G.Visicato, *Early Dynastic Administrative Tablets of Šuruppak*, IUON *Series Maior* VI, Napoli 1994 |
| TLAT | P-Steinkeller-J.N.Postgate, *Third-Millennium Legal and Administrative Texts in the Iraq Museum*, Baghdad, Winona Lake 1992 |
| TMH I-II | A.Pohl, *Texte und Materialien der Frau Professor Hilprecht Collection of Babylonian Antiquities im Eigentum der Universitat Jena* (Leipzig) I-II |
| TSŠ | R.Jestin, *Tablettes sumériennes de Šuruppak conservèes au Musée de Stamboul*, Paris 1937 |
| *Unger* | M.Lambert, *Quatre nouveaux contrats de l'époque de Shuruppak*, in (M.Lurker ed.), *In memoriam Eckhard Unger. Beiträge zu Geschichte, Kultur und Religion des Alten Orients*, Baden-Baden 1971 |
| Waetzoldt, UNT | H.Waetzoldt, *Untersuchugen zur neusumerischen textilindustrie*, Roma 1972 |

| | |
|---|---|
| WF | A.Deimel, *Die Inschriften von Fara III. Wirtschaftstexte aus Fara*, WVDOG 45, Leipzig 1924 |
| ZATU | M.W.Green-H.J.Nissen, *Zeichenliste der Archaischen Texte aus Uruk*, Berlin 1987 |

## LIST OF SIGNS

The reading of the signs in this volume is that of Fr.Ellermeyer, *Sumerische Glossar*, Göttingen 1979, with the following additions:

| | |
|---|---|
| $addir_x$ | LAK 524.A.SI |
| *$bala_x$* | LAK 20 |
| $bil_x$ | PAP.GIŠ.NE |
| $galla_x$ | TE |
| *$lum_x$* | ZU.ZU.SAR |
| $nar_x$ | LAK 244 |
| $nigin_x$ | LAK 358 |
| *$su_x$* | MUŠ |
| $tag_x$ | DÚB |
| $tigi_x$ | BALAG |

## CONCORDANCES

| | | | | | |
|---|---|---|---|---|---|
| **1** | TSŠ 86 | **33** | TSŠ 164 | **65** | WF 88 |
| **2** | WF 65 | **34** | TSŠ 261 | **66** | TSŠ 837 |
| **3** | WF 66 | **35** | WF 107 | **67** | TSŠ 928 |
| **4** | WF 70 | **36** | WF 41 | **68** | WF 53 |
| **5** | WF 73 | **37** | NTSŠ 569 | **69** | TSŠ 102 |
| **6** | WF 74 | **38** | WF 84 | **70** | WF 58 |
| **7** | TSŠ 494 | **39** | WF 86 | **71** | WF 51 |
| **8** | TSŠ 400 | **40** | WF 85 | **72** | TSŠ 100 |
| **9** | TSŠ 7 | **41** | TSŠ 442 | **73** | WF 56 |
| **10** | TSŠ 150 | **42** | NTSŠ 141 | **74** | WF 45 |
| **11** | WF 71 | **43** | NTSŠ 157 | **75** | TSŠ 521 |
| **12** | WF 72 | **44** | NTSŠ 276 | **76** | TSŠ 526 |
| **13** | WF 75 | **45** | NTSŠ 296 | **77** | WF 50 |
| **14** | WF 76 | **46** | TSŠ 78 | **78** | WF 43 |
| **15** | WF 106 | **47** | TSŠ 93 | **79** | WF 44 |
| **16** | WF 61 | **48** | TSŠ 821 | **80** | WF 60 |
| **17** | TSŠ 58 | **49** | WF 64 | **81** | WF 57 |
| **18** | TSŠ 570 | **50** | WF 80 | **82** | TSŠ 101 |
| **19** | WF 77 | **51** | WF 79 | **83** | TSŠ 645 |
| **20** | TSŠ 65 | **52** | TSŠ 209 | **84** | NTSŠ 213 |
| **21** | NTSŠ 65+ | **53** | TSŠ 210 | **85** | NTSŠ 234 |
| **22** | WF 87 | **54** | TSŠ 160 | **86** | NTSŠ 256 |
| **23** | WF 67 | **55** | TSŠ 684 | **87** | TSŠ 486 |
| **24** | WF 68 | **56** | CT 50, 10 | **88** | TSŠ 53 |
| **25** | WF 69 | **57** | CT 50, 11 | **89** | WF 52 |
| **26** | WF 62 | **58** | NTSŠ 273 | **90** | TSŠ 832 |
| **27** | WF 91 | **59** | WF 55 | **91** | NTSŠ 250 |
| **28** | TSŠ 158 | **60** | NTSŠ 140 | **92** | TSŠ 112 |
| **29** | WF 78 | **61** | WF 90 | **93** | WF 54 |
| **30** | TSŠ 130 | **62** | WF 89 | **94** | NTSŠ 147 |
| **31** | TSŠ 237 | **63** | TSŠ 3 | **95** | WF 48 |
| **32** | TSŠ 667 | **64** | TSŠ 723 | **96** | WF 46 |

| | | | | | |
|---|---|---|---|---|---|
| **97** | WF 47 | **131** | TSŠ 344 | **165** | WF 8 |
| **98** | TSŠ 230 | **132** | WF 18 | **166** | WF 2 |
| **99** | TSŠ 463 | **133** | TSŠ 104 | **167** | WF 10 |
| **100** | TSŠ 568 | **134** | WF 15 | **168** | TSŠ 362 |
| **101** | TSŠ 482 | **135** | NTSŠ 165 | **169** | TSŠ 134 |
| **102** | WF 59 | **136** | TSŠ 127+9 | **170** | WF 23 |
| **103** | TSŠ 962 | **137** | TSŠ 115 | **171** | TSŠ 131 |
| **104** | WF 143 | **138** | TSŠ 222 | **173** | WF 105 |
| **105** | NTSŠ 238 | **139** | NTSŠ 444 | **174** | TSŠ 8 |
| **106** | WF 49 | **140** | WF 12 | **175** | TSŠ 113 |
| **107** | NTSŠ 162 | **141** | WF 26 | **176** | TSŠ 2 |
| **108** | TSŠ 91 | **142** | WF 28 | **177** | TSŠ 794 |
| **109** | TSŠ 506 | **143** | WF 124 | **178** | TSŠ 567 |
| **110** | TSŠ 133 | **144** | WF 1 | **179** | TSŠ 15 |
| **111** | TSŠ 274 | **145** | WF 3 | **180** | TSŠ 618 |
| **112** | TSŠ 930 | **146** | WF 16 | **181** | TSŠ 45 |
| **113** | TSŠ 242 | **147** | WF 27 | **182** | WF 99 |
| **114** | TSŠ 758 | **148** | TSŠ 668 | **183** | TSŠ 574 |
| **115** | WF 22 | **149** | TSŠ 704 | **184** | WF 104 |
| **116** | WF 25 | **150** | WF 19 | **185** | TSŠ 245 |
| **117** | NTSŠ 496 | **151** | TSŠ 173 | **186** | DP 34 |
| **118** | TSŠ 64 | **152** | TSŠ 532 | **187** | WF 95 |
| **119** | NTSŠ 169 | **153** | NTSŠ 211 | **188** | CT 50, 1 |
| **120** | TSŠ 107 | **154** | TSŠ 106 | **189** | NTSŠ 114 |
| **121** | TSŠ 1 | **155** | WF 14 | **190** | TSŠ 894 |
| **122** | WF 7 | **156** | WF 11 | **191** | TSŠ 783 |
| **123** | TSŠ 14 | **157** | WF 21 | **192** | WF 98 |
| **124** | WF 9 | **158** | TSŠ 52 | **193** | WF 102 |
| **125** | WF 13 | **159** | TSŠ 498 | **194** | TSŠ 249 |
| **126** | NTSŠ 205 | **160** | WF 123 | **195** | WF 100 |
| **127** | WF 5 | **161** | NTSŠ 244 | **196** | WF 97 |
| **128** | WF 6 | **162** | WF 29 | **197** | WF 92 |
| **129** | WF 24 | **163** | WF 20 | **198** | WF 94 |
| **130** | WF 17 | **164** | WF 4 | **199** | WF 101 |

| | | | | | |
|---|---|---|---|---|---|
| **200** | WF 93 | 78 | **46** | 292 | **209** |
| **201** | Š 768 | 86 | **1** | 344 | **131** |
| **202** | Š 935 | 91 | **108** | 362 | **168** |
| **203** | TSŠ 554 | 93 | **47** | 400 | **8** |
| **204** | TSŠ 780 | 100 | **72** | 442 | **41** |
| **205** | TSŠ 613 | 101 | **82** | 463 | **99** |
| **206** | TSŠ 501 | 102 | **69** | 467 | **216** |
| **207** | TSŠ 993 | 104 | **133** | 482 | **101** |
| **208** | WF 96 | 106 | **154** | 486 | **87** |
| **209** | TSŠ 292 | 107 | **120** | 494 | **7** |
| **210** | TSŠ 765 | 112 | **92** | 498 | **159** |
| **211** | TSŠ 931 | 113 | **175** | 501 | **206** |
| **212** | TSŠ 49 | 115 | **137** | 506 | **109** |
| **213** | CT 50, 3 | 127 | **136** | 521 | **75** |
| **214** | TSŠ 525 | 130 | **30** | 525 | **214** |
| **215** | WF 103 | 131 | **171** | 526 | **76** |
| **216** | TSŠ 467 | 133 | **110** | 532 | **152** |
| **217** | WF 99* | 134 | **169** | 554 | **203** |
| | | 150 | **10** | 567 | **178** |
| TSŠ 1 | **121** | 158 | **28** | 568 | **100** |
| 2 | **176** | 160 | **54** | 570 | **18** |
| 3 | **63** | 164 | **33** | 574 | **183** |
| 7 | **9** | 173 | **151** | 613 | **205** |
| 8 | **174** | 181 | **172** | 618 | **180** |
| 9 | **136** | 209 | **52** | 645 | **83** |
| 14 | **123** | 210 | **53** | 667 | **32** |
| 15 | **179** | 222 | **138** | 668 | **148** |
| 45 | **181** | 230 | **98** | 684 | **55** |
| 49 | **212** | 237 | **31** | 704 | **149** |
| 52 | **158** | 242 | **113** | 723 | **64** |
| 53 | **88*** | 245 | **185** | 758 | **114** |
| 58 | **17** | 249 | **194** | 765 | **210** |
| 64 | **118** | 261 | **34** | 780 | **204** |
| 65 | **20** | 274 | **111** | 783 | **191** |

| | | | | | | |
|---|---|---|---|---|---|---|
| 794 | **177** | | | | 46 | **96** |
| 821 | **48** | WF | 1 | **144** | 47 | **97** |
| 832 | **90** | | 2 | **166** | 48 | **95** |
| 837 | **66** | | 3 | **145** | 49 | **106** |
| 894 | **190** | | 4 | **164** | 50 | **77** |
| 928 | **67** | | 5 | **127** | 51 | **71** |
| 930 | **112** | | 6 | **128** | 52 | **89** |
| 931 | **211** | | 7 | **122** | 53 | **68** |
| 933 | **207** | | 8 | **165** | 54 | **93** |
| 962 | **103** | | 9 | **124** | 55 | **59** |
| | | | 10 | **167** | 56 | **73** |
| NTSŠ 65+ | **21** | | 11 | **156** | 57 | **81** |
| 114 | **189** | | 12 | **140** | 58 | **70** |
| 140 | **60** | | 13 | **125** | 59 | **102** |
| 141 | **42** | | 14 | **155** | 60 | **80** |
| 147 | **94** | | 15 | **134** | 61 | **16** |
| 157 | **43** | | 16 | **146** | 62 | **26** |
| 162 | **107** | | 17 | **130** | 64 | **49** |
| 165 | **135** | | 18 | **132** | 65 | **2** |
| 169 | **119** | | 19 | **150** | 66 | **3** |
| 205 | **126** | | 20 | **163** | 67 | **23** |
| 211 | **153** | | 21 | **157** | 68 | **24** |
| 213 | **84** | | 22 | **115** | 69 | **25** |
| 234 | **85** | | 23 | **170** | 70 | **4** |
| 238 | **105** | | 24 | **129** | 71 | **1** |
| 244 | **161** | | 25 | **116** | 72 | **12** |
| 250 | **91** | | 26 | **141** | 73 | **5** |
| 256 | **86** | | 27 | **147** | 74 | **6** |
| 273 | **58** | | 28 | **142** | 75 | **13** |
| 276 | **44** | | 29 | **162** | 76 | **14** |
| 296 | **45** | | 41 | **36** | 77 | **19** |
| 444 | **139** | | 43 | **78** | 78 | **29** |
| 496 | **117** | | 44 | **79** | 79 | **51** |
| 569 | **37** | | 45 | **74** | 80 | **50** |

| | | | |
|---|---|---|---|
| 84 | **38** | DP 34 | **186** |
| 85 | **40** | | |
| 86 | **39** | Š 768 | **201** |
| 87 | **22** | Š 935 | **202** |
| 88 | **65** | | |
| 89 | **62** | | |
| 90 | **61** | | |
| 91 | **27** | | |
| 92 | **197** | | |
| 93 | **200** | | |
| 94 | **198** | | |
| 95 | **187** | | |
| 96 | **208** | | |
| 97 | **196** | | |
| 98 | **192** | | |
| 99 | **182** | | |
| 99* | **217** | | |
| 100 | **195** | | |
| 101 | **199** | | |
| 102 | **193** | | |
| 103 | **215** | | |
| 104 | **184** | | |
| 105 | **173** | | |
| 106 | **15** | | |
| 107 | **35** | | |
| 123 | **160** | | |
| 124 | **143** | | |
| 143 | **104** | | |
| | | | |
| CT 50, 1 | **188** | | |
| CT 50, 3 | **213** | | |
| CT 50, 10 | **56** | | |
| CT 50, 11 | **57** | | |

# INTRODUCTION

The analysis made by the author in the first volume of the Fara texts emphasized the centralized structure of the administration of Šuruppak during the ED IIIa period (cf. *Šuruppak*, pp.1-9). This administration appears to have been organized in at least two principal centres; the é-gal and the é-uru, literally, "the palace" and "the city". The first was staffed by the courtiers and those responsible for control and organization while the latter was essentially connected with artisan and productive activity. From the texts examined (texts **1-13**, cf. *Šuruppak*, pp.28-93), the é-gal centre was structured in a series of administrative units, each of which was headed by an ugula (cf. *ibidem*, comm. on **2-3**). In addition, we know that the galas (cf. *ibidem*, comm. on **6**), the nimgirs (cf. *ibidem*, comm on **4** and **5**) and the dam-gàrs (cf **1** r. II 6-III 2) were attached to this centre. These officials, together with their subordinates, must have been under their respective corporation heads. As well as these but at a higher level, there were the dub-sar (cf. *Šuruppak*, comm. on texts **7** and **8**) whose task seems to have been that of control and organization. At a lower level, there were the lú-ri-ri-ga (cf. *ibidem*, comm. on text **1**) who were probably employed in agricultural work in the state lands. The whole centre, on the basis of the documentation contained in texts **1-13**, seems to have given employment to no less than two thousand people (cf. *ibidem*, p. 36).

The second centre, the one called é-uru, was composed essentially of personnel connected with the handcrafts, with animal breeding, with river navigation and boats and with fishing as can be deduced from the professional names which characterize the beneficiaries of the allocations mentioned in the II group of the barley texts (texts **14-37**, cf. *ibidem*, pp. 94-96). The texts of this group mention the engars, absent in the texts of the I group, in the role of the officials who were responsible for the rations of barley.

If the analysis of the above-mentioned texts has enabled us to identify these two main centres, it has revealed rather little about the existence and characteristics of the central offices and the intermediate structures linked to these centres. These offices must have constituted the connective tissue of the entire administrative organization. The study of two groups of texts regarding personnel, one regarding the dumu-dumu **(181-186)** and the other the guruš **(187-196)**, which are analysed in the first chapter of this book, has enabled us to identify the officials responsible for a series of offices linked both to the administration and to the production of goods and services. The classification of the officials who provided personnel for the recruitment mentioned in these two groups of texts has enabled us to add a series of tesserae to the mosaic we had already tried to reconstruct. This new and more up-to-date picture still leaves many aspects completely in the dark and has margins of uncertainty due, on the one hand, to the conciseness of the administrative documentation of Fara consisting almost entirely of registers listing people who receive goods, and on the other hand, to the widespread homonymity which is a feature of the onomasticon of the officials mentioned in the texts, not always indentifiable with certainty because they lack the characterizing element (this is a professional name or the name of the centre or of the official who he is subordinate).

In some cases, even the presence of the characterizing element does not always render such an identification certain. It is, in fact, possible that the same official is described with a different characterizing element in different texts. For example, dumu-nun-šita is mentioned in some texts (**10** v. V 5-6; **65** r. I 2-3; TSŠ 548 r. I' 3'-4'; WF 148 r. II 1-2) as PA-AN/$^{d}$sùd, while in others (**47** r. II 8-9; **127** r. IV 4-5) he is described as IB. In the same way, KA-lugal-da-zi is described in some texts as lú-má-gal-gal (**121** r. IV 7-8; **132** r. VI 9-19; **135** r. V 4'-5') and in others as engar (**19** v. VIII 11-12; IX 6; **34** r. III 3); it is only the mention of this anthroponym as engar lú-má-gal-gal in **29** v. II 4-6 which has enabled us to establish that he was the same official.

It can even happen that the same anthroponym is followed in one text by the name of one official and in another by a different one; identification in this case is possible only if we can establish that the two officials described by the anthroponym are, in their turn, related to one another by subordination. For example, we can identify lam-ma UR.UR mentioned in **127** v. IV 7-8 with lam-ma mes-$u_4$-ba of **7** r. II' 7-8 only because in **19** r. VIII 12-13 and in **29** r. IV 7-8 mes-$u_4$-ba UR.UR is mentioned which indicates that mes-$u_4$-ba is a subordinate of UR.UR, a high-ranking official described elsewhere as maškim maškim-$gi_4$.

Another possible source of confusion arises from the custom the compilers of the tablets had of abbreviating both the anthroponyms and the professional names. For example, the anthroponym abzu-ta-mud is abbreviated in some cases as AB-(ta)-mud which, with the possible reading of ès-(ta)-mud, would be distinguished from the previous one; but only the mention in two parallel texts of the name of this official in both variants (cf. **115** r. II 10-11: AB-ta-mud na-gada; **117** r. III 4-5: abzu-(ta)-mud na-gada) has enabled us to establish the identity of the two anthroponyms.

Finally, another possibility of confusion arises from these abbreviations in the case of name types like PN Prof.N where no variants exist. This sequence normally indicates that the official exercises the profession indicated by his personal name; but often this sequence is an abbreviation of PN Prof.$N_1$ Prof.$N_2$ which indicates that the official mentioned is a Prof.$N_1$ in the service of Prof.$N_2$. As examples of this practice we have é-$^{d}$anzu who in **23** r. IV 1-2 is followed by the professional name sukkal and in the parallel text in **25** r. II 4-6 by that of lú-má sukkal[1] ; and also amar-kù who in **117** r. II 1-2 followed by sanga-GAR and in the parallel passages **115** r. I 9-11 and **116** r. IV 15-17 by SAL.UŠ sanga-GAR; and finally, amar-$^{d}$IB who in **24** v. I 7-8 is followed by enku and in **23** v. IV 12-14 by su-$ku_6$ enku.

Only the particular technique of compilation of the texts which envisaged, for each administrative operation or transaction, the compilation of primary, intermediate and general summary documents where whole sections are parallel and a series of correspondences between the items recorded (cf. *Šuruppak*, pp.21-26) have enabled us, through the identification of a long list of variants, to overcome many of the difficulties and ambiguities mentioned above.

The new data added to the information acquired in the previous study and to elements drawn from the remaining documentation have enabled us to identify a series of structures connected to é-gal and the é-uru, like, for example, the é-géme, the é-gal-nimgir, the é-gala-mah, the KISAL, the é-enku, the cattle breeding centres and the é-gal-dam-gàr. All of these structures must have constituted the organizational complex of the administration of Šuruppak between ED II and ED III. In the conclusion, we have proposed, in schematic form, a possible organizational chart.

---

1 As a general rule, when in the Fara texts the professional name is not preceded by an anthroponym it means that the scribe was referring to the gal-Prof.N, that is, the highest ranking official of that corporation (cf. *Šuruppak*, p. 63).

# CHAPTER I

## The Recruitment Texts

## §.1 The dumu-dumu texts (181-186)

**A**) The study of a particular group of texts concerning the personnel described as dumu-dumu šà-é-gal "personnel of the palace administration" has enabled us to establish precisely both the number of the administrative units and the average number of persons employed in each. Consequently, we have been able to verify and define, at least in rough outline, the reconstruction presented regarding the size of the palace administration (cf. *Šuruppak*, p.34).

This group of six texts has a series of reciprocal correlations analogous to those already found both in the texts published in *Šuruppak* and in a fair part of the remaining documentation of Fara. These reciprocal correlations demonstrate, also for this group of texts, the particular practice of document compilation adopted by the scribes of Šuruppak in that period (cf. *Šuruppak*, pp.21-24; 30-36; 96-104).

It should be noted that two texts, **182** and **184,** the only ones whose findspot is known, come from the site XVII c,d situated in the extreme northern part of the *tell* (cf. Martin, *Fara*, p.88). On the basis of the correlations indicated in the notes on the text, this is also thought to be the provenance of the other four tablets.

### 181 (TSŠ 45)

r. I 1) [ ] [dumu-dumu]
2) [lú-lu]m-[ma]
3) [kínda](1)
4) [ ] [ur-$^{d}$nin$^{?}$]-PA(2)
5) [ ] [lú-é-zi$^{?}$]
6) [a-zu$_5$$^{?}$](3)

II 1) [x+]10 har-tu-[$^{d}$s]ùd(4)
2) 30 é-ki-ba maškim(5)
3) 19 sag-nar$_x$
4) [x] lá 1 ba-za$_7$
5) [ ] mes-[ki-na$^{?}$]

6) lú-HAR

III 1) 29 é-[n]u$^{!}$-kur-[s]i[6]

2) 25 lú-na-nam

3) sukkal[7]

4) 29 šubur[8]

5) 29 A[N].URUDU-s[i]

6) [sagi][9]

IV 1) 20 NI.NI[9]

2) 19 dub-hul-tar

3) agrig

4) [x+]11 nin-unken[10]

5) 25 šubur

6) muhaldim[11]

7) 18 DI-utu[12]

V 1) 20 $^{d}$sùd-ur-sag[13]

2) [10$^{?}$+]9 ur-é-gal[14]

3) 19 é-UD-nu-dib

4) lú-ad[15]

5) [x+]10 AK

v. I 1) nar[16]

2) 20 KA-zi-da

3) munu$_4$[17]

4) 10 lugal-PA-du$_{10}$

5) lú-di

6) 23 NI.NI

7) sa-HAR[18]

II-IV blank

V 1) [an-šè-gú] [360$^{?}$+]120 [dumu-]dumu

2) [šà-é]-gal

(1) 2 (**182** r. I 1; **184** r. I 1-2); 3(**183** r. I 1-2); 78 (**185** r. I 1-2).
(2) 1 (**184** r. I 1-3); 1 (**183** r. I 3).
(3) 2 (**182** r. I 2).
(4) 3 (**184** r. I 4); 4 (**182** r I 3; **183** r. I 4); 72 (**185** r. I 3).
(5) 1 (**184** r. I 5); 3 (**183** r. I 5); 6 (**182** r. I 4).
(6) 77 (**185** r. I 4).
(7) 4 (**184** r. II 1); 4(**183** r. II 1).
(8) 2 (**184** r. II 2-3); 2(**183** r. II 2); 67 (**185** r II 1).
(9) 67 (**185** r. II 2).
(10) 2 (**184** r. II 6-7; **183** r. II 3): 4 (**182** r. I 5-6); 65 (**185** r. II 3).
(11) 3 (**184** r. II 4; **183** r. II 4).
(12). 2 (**184** r. II 8); 3(**183** r. II 5); 113 (**185** r. II 4); [x+]2 (**186** r. I 1-3).
(13) 1 (**184** r. III 1); 4 (**182** r. II 1); 6 (**183** r. II 6); [ ] (**186** r. I 4).
(14) 2 (**182** r. II 3; **184** r. III 3); 25 (**186** r. II 1-2).
(15) 3 (**184** r. III 2; **182** r. II 4).
(16) 4 (**182** r. II 5); 6 (**184** r. III 6); 20 (**186** r. II 3-4).
(17) 3 (**184** r. III 5); 12 (**186** r. II 5-6).
(18) 2 (**182** r. II 6-7); 1 NI.NI nar (**184** v. II 4-5).

The left-hand edge of this tablet is partially destroyed; for this reason, in the first column of the recto only one part of the sign LUM in the second line and the sign PA in the third line are legible; all the other lines are totally lost. In the last column of the verso only some numbers which formed part of the summary survive together with the signs DUMU and GAL.

While the integration of r. I 1-3, [x dumu-dumu] [lú]-lum-[ma] [x ur-$^{d}$nin]-PA, seems fairly certain[2] from a comparison with other texts of the group (notes 1-2), the integration of r. I 5-6 lú-é-zi a-$zu_5$ and of r.II 5 mes-[ki-na] lú-HAR seem less

---

2 Lu-Lumma as ugula-kínda is attested in **11** r. VI 9-10; v. I 1'-2'; **13** r. IV 7-8; and in TSŠ 732 r. III 1-2; and as ugula (kínda) in **10** v. III 2; IV 1; and in **11** r. I 4; II 11. From the documentation which has survived, however, we are not able to determine the profession of ur-$^{d}$nin-PA.

certain; the former is supported by a comparison with **182** r. I 2 (note 3) which mentions Lu-Ezi in second position[3] and the latter by the mention of Meskina lú-HAR in one of the primary texts concerning barley in the I group (**13** v. V 4) as the official whose subordinate is Ageštin; Meskina is thus to be identified as an ugula of the é-gal. TSŠ r. III 1 copies é-⌈X⌉-kur-⌈X⌉ but the comparison with **185** r. I 4, [ ]-si, suggests the emendation é-[n]u-kur-[s]i. This foreman is mentioned in the primary documentation **9-13** as ugula-sukkal (cf. *infra*, p.23). In addition, the integration of r. III 6 A[N].URUDU-[s]i [sagi] appears to be certain because this official is mentioned in **3** v. I 5'-6' and several times in **9-13**.

The summary is, for the most part, lost but from the sum of the surviving items, the personnel listed in the text must have numbered about 500.

### 182 (WF 99)

r. I 1) 2 lú-lum-ma(1)
2) 2 lú-é-zi(2)
3) 4 har-tu-$^{d}$sùd(3)
4) 6 é-ki-ba(4)
5) 4 nin-[u]nken
6) muhaldim(5)

II 1) 4 $^{d}$sùd-ur-sag(6)
2) 6 lugal-ezen(7)
3) 3 ur-é-gal(8)
4) 3 é-UD-nu-dib(9)
5) 4 AK(10)
6) 2 NI.NI
7) ⌈s⌉a-HAR(11)

III 1) 3 dar-da

---

3 This official is mentioned several times in the primary documentation of the first group (cf. **9-13**).

2) ugula lú-di

3) 5 lú-pà(12)

4) 3 é-ki-gal-la!(13)

5) 5 KA-dsùd-da-zi(14)

6) 6 AK-dsùd(15)

IV 1) 2 a-HU.HA(16)

2) 4 é-nu-si

3) ⸢ad⸣-KID(17)

4) 4 é-kur-ra(18)

5) 10 $uru_{18}$

5) [lú-n]ab(19)

v. I-III blank

IV 1) blank

2) 79 guruš

3) zì-ba

4) 6 (bariga) 3 (bàn) 5 sìla

5) 5 sìla šu-ba-ti

(1) **184** r. I 1-2; 3 (**183** r. I 1-2); 78 (**185** r. I 1-2); [ ] (**181** r. I 1-2).

(2) [ ] (**181** r. I 4-5 ?

(3) 3(**184** r. I 4); 4 (**183** r. I 4); 72 (**185** r. I 3); [x+]10 (**181** r. II 1).

(4) 1 (**184** r. I 5); 3 (**183** r. I 5); 30 (**181** r. II 2).

(5) 2 (**184** r. II 6-7; **183** r. II 3); 65 (**185** r. I 3); [x+]11 (**181** r. IV 4).

(6) 1 (**184** r. III 1); 6 (**183** r. II 6); 20 (**181** r. V 1); [ ] (**186** r. I 4).

(7) 2 (**184** r. III 4).

(8) **184** r. III 3; [10?+]9 (**181** r: V 2); 25 (**186** r. II 1-2).

(9) **184** r. III 2; 19 (**181** r. V 3-4).

(10) 6 (**184** r. III 6); [x+]10 (**181** r. V 5); 20 (**186** r. II 3-4).

(11) 23 (**181** v. I 6-7); 1 NI.NI nar (**184** v. II 5).

(12) 1 (**184** r. IV 1).

(13) 2 (**184** r. IV 2).

(14) **184** r. IV 3.

(15) 4 (**184** r. IV 4).

(16) [ ] A.HU.HA íl-šitim (**184** v. I 2-3).

(17) 1 (**184** v. I 4-5).

(18) [ ] [é]-kur-ra bahar$_4$ (**184** v. I 7-II 1).

(19) 5 (**184** v. II 2-3).

r. III 4: A.Deimel (cf. WF, p.69) reads é-ki-gal-si (cf. also **184** r. IV 2); but this anthroponym is not mentioned elsewhere in the documentation of Fara. It should be read é-ki-gal-la and the person identified with the ugula zadim mentioned in **12** r. V 8'-9'.

r. IV 3: A.Deimel reads ugula é-eren, an official never mentioned in the Fara texts. In fact, the two signs which he saw as separate are part of one sign, AD. The ugula ad-KID Enusi is mentioned several times in **9-13** as well as in **184** r. IV 4-5.

r. IV 6: the integration derives from a comparison with the parallel passage in **184** (v. II 2-3).

## 183 (TSŠ 574)

r. I 1) 3** dumu-dumu
2) lú-lum-ma(1)
3) 1* ur-$^{d}$nin-PA(2)
4) 4 har-tu-[$^{d}$s]ùd(3)
5) 3 é-ki-ba(4)

II 1) 4*** lú-na-nam(5)
2) 2** šubur(6)
3) 2 nin-unken-a(7)
4) 3 šubur(8)
5) 3 DI-utu(9)
6) 6 $^{d}$sùd-ur-sag(10)

III 1) lú-šu$^{!}$-bad

2) a-hu-ti

3) dub-sar

(1) 2 (**182** r. I 1; **184** r. I 1-2); 78 (**185** r. I 1-2); [ ] (**181** r. I 1-2).

(2) **184** r. I 3; [ ] (**181** r. II 3).

(3) **182** r. I 3; 3 (**184** r. I 4); 72 (**185** r. I 3); [x+]10 (**181** r. I 1).

(4) 1 (**184** r. I 5); 6 (**182** r. I 4); 30 (**181** r. II 2).

(5) **184** r. II 1; 25 (**181** r. III 2).

(6) **184** r. II 2-3; 65[+2] (**185** r. II 1).

(7) **184** r. II 6-7; 4 (**182** r. I 5-6); 65 (**185** r. II 3); [x+]11 (**181** r. IV 4).

(8) 3 (**184** r. II 4); 25 (**181** r. IV 5).

(9) 2 (**184** r. II 8); 18 (**181** r. IV 7); 113 (**185** r. II 4); [x+]2 (**186** r. I 1-3).

(10) 1 (**184** r. III 1); 4 (**182** r. II 1); 20 (**181** r. V 1); [ ] (**186** r. I 4).

r. III 1: TSŠ has lú-ŠÈ-bad, a clause which it is difficult to interpret. Even though we had no photograph of the text, we believe that the sign copied ŠÈ is really ŠU (for the mentions and the meaning of šu-bad in the Fara texts, cf. *Šuruppak*, p.181, note 56). The scribe Ahuti could have been the compiler of the tablet, but on the basis of the correlations between the dumu-dumu texts and the guruš documents which will be examined in the next section, we believe that he is the official to whom the term šu-bad refers. He was probably also in charge of the sustenance for the men under his supervision.

## 184 (WF 104)

r. I 1) 2 dumu-dumu

2) lú-lum-ma(1)

3) 1 ur-$^{d}$nin-PA(2)

4) 3 har-[t]u-$^{d}$sùd(3)

5) 1 é-ki-ba(4)

6) 4

II 1) lú-na-nam(5)

2) 2 šubur
3) sagi(6)
4) 3 šubur
5) muhaldim(7)
6) 2 nin-unken(7)
7) muhaldim
8) 2 DI-utu(8)

III 1) 1 $^{d}$sùd-ur-sag(9)
2) 3 é-UD-nu-dib(10)
3) 2 ur-é-gal(11)
4) 2 lugal-ezen(12)
5) 3 KA-zi-da(13)
6) 6 AK(14)

IV 1) 1 lú-pà(15)
2) 2 é-ki-gal-l[a](16)
3) 5 KA-$^{d}$sùd-da-zi(17)
4) 4 AK-$^{d}$sùd
5) t[úg$^{?}$-du$_{8}$$^{?}$](18)

v. I 1) [ ]
2) [ ] A.HU.[HA]
3) íl-šitim(19)
4) 1 é-nu.si
5) ad-KID(20)
6) [ ]
7) [ ] [é]-kur-ra

II 1) bah[ar]$_{4}$(21)
2) 5 ⌜uru$_{18}$⌝
3) lú-nab(22)
4) 1 NI.NI
5) nar(23)

III blank

IV 1) an-šè-gú 59 ⌜dumu-dumu⌝

2) [šà] ⌜é?⌝-⌜gal?⌝

(1) 2 (**182** r. I 1); 3 (**183** r. I 1-2); 78 (**185** r. I 1-2) [ ] (**181** r. I 1-2).

(2) 1*(**183** r. I 3); [ ] (**181** r. I 3).

(3) 4 (**182** r. I 3; **183** r. I 4); 72 (**185** r. I 3); [x+]10 (**181** r. II 1).

(4) 3 (**183** r. I 5); 6 (**182** r. I 4); 30 (**181** r. II 2).

(5) 4(**183** r. II 1); 25 (**181** r. III 2).

(6) 2(**183** r. II 2); 29 (**181** r. III 4-5); 65[+2] (**185** r. II 1).

(7) 2 (**183** r. II 3); 4 (**182** r. I 5-6); 65 (**185** r. II 3); [x+]2 (**186** r. I 1-3); [x+]11 (**181** r. IV 4).

(8) 3 (**183** r. II 4); 18 (**181** r. IV 7); 113 (**185** r. II 4); [ ] (**186** r. I 4).

(9) 4 (**182** r. II 1); 6 (**183** r. II 6); 20 (**181** r. V 1).

(10) **182** r. II 4; 19 (**181** r. V 3).

(11) **182** r. II 3; 25 (**186** r. II 1-2); [10?+]9 (**181** r. V 2).

(12) 6 (**182** r. II 2).

(13) 12 (**186** r. II 5-6); 20 (**181** v. I 2-3).

(14) 4 (**182** r. II 5); 20 (**186** r. II 3-4); [x+]10 (**181** r. V 5).

(15) 5 (**182** r. III 3).

(16) 3 (**182** r. III 4).

(17) **182** r. III 5.

(18) 6 (**182** r. III 6).

(19) 2 (**182** r. IV 1).

(20) 4 (**182** r. IV 2-3)

(21) 4 (**182** r. IV 4).

(22) 10 (**182** r. IV 5-6).

(23) NI.NI sa-HAR: 2 (**182** r. II 6-7); 23 (**181** v. I 6-7).

r. IV 6: The integration is proposed on the basis of a comparison with **96** r. III-IV: AK-$^{d}$sùd túg-$du_{8}$.

v. I 3: We have considered the term íl as the professional name of A.HU.HA, a subordinate of the (gal)-šitim. But it is possible that íl is a personal name (for the mention of the personal name íl in the Fara documentation cf. Pomponio, *Prosopografia*, p. 125-126). In this case, the professional name šitim must refer to íl. Because A.HU.HA is an ugula (cf, *infra*, p.24) it is possible to identify íl with the gal-šitim, on whom A.HU.HA as ugula-šitim depends.

v. IV 2: WF reads am[a]-[ ], but the form of the sign and especially a comparison with the colophon of **181** suggests a different reading.

## 185 (TSŠ 245)

r I 1) 78 dumu-dumu
2) lú-lum-ma(1)
3) 72 har-tu-$^{d}$sùd(2)
4) 77 [é-nu-ku]r-si(3)

II 1) 62[+5] šubur(4)
2) 67 NI.NI(5)
3) 65 nin-unken-a(6)
4) 113 DI-utu(7)

v- I blank

II 1) [an]-šè-[g]ú
2) 539 dumu-dumu
3) 7 im-ru

(1) 2 (**182** r. I 1; **184** r. I 1-2); 3 (**183** r. I 1-2); [x] (**181** r. I 1-2).

(2) 3 (**184** r. I 4); 4 (**182** r. I 3; **183** r. I 4); [x+]10 (**181** r. II 1).

(3) 29 (**181** r. III 1).

(4) 2 (**184** r. II 2-3; **183** r. II 2); 29 (**181** r. III 4).

(5) 20 (**181** r. IV 1).

(6) 2 (**184** r. II 6-7; **183** r. II 3); 4 (**182** r. I 5-6); [x+]11 (**181** r. IV 4).

(7) 2 (**184** r. II 8); 3 (**183** r. II 5); 18 (**181** r. IV 7); [x+]2 (**186** r. I 1-3).

r. I 4: the integration [é-nu-ku]r-si is suggested by a comparison with **181** r. III 1 where this official precedes in order both šubur and NI.NI.

v. II 3: the term im-ru has been translated by Th. Jacobsen as "clan"; he derives it from the same root as the term im-ri-a, akk. *kimtu*, "family" (MSL 5, 17, 117). A. Falkenstein has translated it as *Gerarkungen*, "district" (cf. D.O.Edzard, *Fara und Salabikh. Die "Wirtschaftstexte"*, ZA 66 [1977], p.173, *sub* TSŠ 245). The bilingual dictionaries of Ebla have im-ru = *pù-a-tu* (cf. MEE IV, p.336, 1338') perhaps derived from the akk. *pāṭu*, *pattu* "district" (suggestion by P.Steinkeller).

## 186 (DP 34)

r. I 1) [x+]2 [d]umu-[du]mu
2) di-[utu] ugula
3) lú-ad(1)
4) [ ] ᵈsùd-[ur]-sag
5) u[gula](2)

II 1) 25 ur-é-gal
2) ugula(3)
3) 20 nar
4) AK(4)
5) 12 munu$_4$
6) KA-z[i-da](5)

v. I 1) [ ][ ]gal?-[ ]
2) [lú?]-di
3) blank?
4) [ba]-DU
5) blank

(1) 2 (**184** r. II 7); 3 (**183** r. II 5); 18 (**181** r. IV 7); 113 (**185** r. II 4).

(2) 1 (**184** r. III 1); 4 (**182** r. II 1); 6 (**183** r. II 6); 20 (**181** r. V 1).

(3) 2 (**182** r. II 3; **184** r. III 3); [10?+]9 (**181** r. V 2).

(4) 4 (**182** r. II 5); 6 (**184** r. III 6); [x+]10 (**181** r. V 5-v. I 1).
(5) 3 (**184** r. III 5); 20 (**181** v. II 2-3).

This is the smallest document of the group and consists in two columns of 5 and 6 lines respectively on the recto; there was probably the same number of columns on the verso. The tablet has reached us without the external part of the left side of the recto but the lacunae can be integrated perfectly from a comparison with **181**, **182** and **184**. The verso where only the first column seems to have been written has large lacunae. The surviving signs gal and di in v. I 1-2 are probably all that remains of the name lugal-pa-$du_{10}$, the ugula lú-di mentioned after KA-zi-da, ugula $munu_4$ in **181** v. I 4-5. In v. I 4, the only surviving sign DU must have been part of the term ba-DU. One cannot exclude that the third line, which from the copy in DP seems to be unwritten, could have included the term dumu-dumu. In both cases there seems to be no doubt about the meaning of the final clause ba-DU; it means that the men for whom the ugulas mentioned in the text were responsible were made available or assigned for the operation to which this group of texts refers.

**B)** All the texts have reciprocal concordances as can be seen from the notes on the texts. The items are listed, with rare exceptions, in the same order. The concordances among the items, however, concern only the anthroponyms; almost never the number which precedes them. This is a slightly different situation from that encountered in the documents of barley, allotment fields, anše and carts analysed in *Šuruppak*. In fact, in the case of these latter texts, two types of correlations were encountered:

a) the corresponding items were listed in the same order and the anthroponyms were generally preceded by an identical number;
b) the corresponding items were, in most cases, not listed in the same order and the anthroponym was not preceded by the same number.

To understand better the type of relationship which exists between the dumu-dumu texts, we present Table 1 which lists all the concordances between them. In brackets, in relation to each item, the number of the dumu-dumu which precedes the anthroponym is shown.

**Table 1**

| 181 | 182 | 183 | 184 | 185 | 186 |
|---|---|---|---|---|---|
| r. I 1-3 (x) | r. I 1 (2 ) | r. I 1-2 (3) | r. I 1-2 (2 ) | r. I 1-2 (78) | |
| r. I 4 (x) | | r. I 3 (1) | r. I 3 (1) | | |
| r. I 5-6 (x) | r. I 2 (2) | | | | |
| r. II 1 (x+10) | r. I 3 (4) | r. I 4 (4) | r. I 4 (4) | r. I 3 (72) | |
| r. II 2 (30) | r. I 4 (6) | r. I 5 (3) | r. I 5 (1) | | |
| r. II 3 (19) | | | | | |
| r. II 4 (x) | | | | | |
| r. II 5-6 (x) | | | | | |
| r. III 1 (29) | | | | r. I 4 (77) | |
| r. III 2-3 (25) | | r. II 1 (4) | r. II 1 (4) | | |
| r. III 4 (x+11) | | r. II 2 (2) | r. II 2-3 (2) | r. II 1 (67?) | |
| r. III 5-6 (29) | | | | | |
| r. IV 1 (20) | | | | r. II 2 (67) | |
| r. IV 2-3 (19) | | | | | |
| r. IV 4 (x+11) | r. I 5-6 (4) | r. II 3 (2) | r. II 6 (2) | r. II 3 (65) | |
| r. IV 5-6 (25) | | r. II 4 (3) | r. II 4-5 (3) | | |
| r. IV 7 (18) | | r. II 5 (3) | r. II 7 (2) | r. II 4 (113) | r. I 1-3 (x+2) |
| r. V 1 (20) | r. II 1 (4) | r. II 6 (6) | r. III 1 (1) | **End of text** | r. I 4 (x) |
| | r. II 2 (6) | **End of text** | r. III 4 (2) | (7 items) | |
| r. V 2 (19?) | r. II 3 (3) | (10 items) | r. III 3 (2) | | r. II 1-2 (20) |
| r. V 3-4 (19) | r. II 4 (3) | | r. III 2 (3) | | |
| r.V5-v.I1(x+10) | r. II 5 (4) | | r. III 6 (6) | | r. II 3-4 (20) |
| v. I 2-3 (20) | | | r. III 5 (3) | | r. II 5-6 (12) |
| v. I 4-5 (10) | | | | | v. I 1-2 (x)? |
| v. I 6-7 (23) | r. II 6-7 (2) | | v. II 4-5 (1) | | **End of text** |
| **End of text** | r. III 1-2 (3) | | | | (6 items) |
| (24 items) | r. III 3 (5) | | r. IV 1 (1) | | |

| | | | | | |
|---|---|---|---|---|---|
| | r. III 4 (3) | | r. IV 2 (2) | | |
| | r. III 5 (5) | | r. IV 3 (5) | | |
| | r. III 6 (6) | | r. IV 4-5 (4) | | |
| | | | v. I 1 (x) | | |
| | r. IV 1(2) | | v. I 2-3 (x) | | |
| | r. IV 2-3 (4) | | v. I 4-6 (1) | | |
| | r. IV 4 (4) | | v. I 7-II 1 (x) | | |
| | r. IV 5-6 (10) | | v. II 2-3 (5) | | |
| | **End of text** | | **End of text** | | |
| | (20 items) | | (25 items) | | |

**Table 1** enables us to make a series of observations:

a) all the items of **183** (10 items), **185** (7 items), **186** (6 items), the first part of **182** (r. I 1-II 7l; 11 items) and the first part of **184** (r. I 1-III 5; 16 items) have correspondences with the items of **181** (24 items). This latter lists six other items (r. II 3; 4; 5-6; III 5-6; IV 2-3) which are not present in the other texts. It should also be noted that two items of **181** (r. III 1;IV 1) have correspondences only in **185**.
b) the nine items listed in the second part of **182** (r. III 1-IV 6) have correspondences only with those of the second part of **184** (r. IV 1-v. II 2).
c) the number which precedes the anthroponym in the items in **182-184** is never, with one exception (**182** r. IV 5-6), more than 6, while in the surviving items of **186** it is the same or more than 12 and in those in **181**, with one exception (v. I 4-5), it is always more than 18. Finally, the number in the seven items of **185** is between 65 and 113.

On the basis of these observations we can draw the following conclusions:

1) **181** is a general summary document which groups together both the items listed in **183**, **186** and in the first parts of **182** and **184** and those from similar texts which have not survived.

2) one other general summary text must have existed which grouped the items of the second parts of **182** and **184**.
3) **182** and **184**, which are largely parallel, must be attributed to a phase of compilation which precedes that of **181**. 18 of the 20 items of **182** have correspondences in **184**; and the two remaining items correspond to two items in **181**. Of the seven items of **184** which are not present in **182**, five have correspondences both with **181** and **183**, one with **181** while the seventh does not correspond to any of the items in the other texts. It is probable that, as we have said, other documents pertaining to this intermediate stage of compilation must have existed which have not survived.
4) **183** should be regarded as the only primary document. In fact, the ten items listed in this text correspond to the first ten of **184**. But it should be noted that the number preceding the anthroponym in the ten items of the text is in five cases (r. I 3; II 1; 2; 3; 4) the same as that of the corresponding items in **184**, and in the remaining five (r. I 1; 4; 5; II 5; 6) it is greater. In addition, in three of the first five cases the number in **183** is followed by oblique wedges which probably means that the operation registered in the text was repeated more than once (cf. *Šuruppak*, p.68). For these reasons, it is probable that **183** was compiled after or at the same time as **184** and must be regarded as an updated summary of preceding documents. These latter which must have been the source from which **184** was drawn must be considered the real primary documents.
5) **186** lists 6 items which correspond in the same order to the same number of items in **181** (r. IV 7-v. I 5). In spite of the lacunae in both texts, the numbers which precede the anthroponyms in these corresponding items, with some slight differences, seem to have the same total. The relationship between the two texts consequently appears to be similar to that which connects **183** with **184**. It is probable, then, that the compilation of **186** was contemporary or immediately prior to that of **181**. On the contrary, the numbers in the items which **186** has in common with **184** and **182** are much higher even though the order is the same. This means that **186** belongs to a phase of compilation subsequent to that of these latter texts.

6) **185** must have a different meaning. As we shall see in the following pages, this text seems to be a census of the staff on duty in some of the administrative units.

**C)** The colophon in all the texts in this group has a summary of the personnel listed. After the summary another clause is added;

**181**: dumu-dumu šà-é-gal, "palace personnel"

**182**: zì-ba 6(b) 3(bàn) 5 sìla šu-ba-ti, "(the summary of) rations of flour (are) 6 bariga 3 bàn and 5 sìla, (the ration) received (by each man is) 5 sìla".

**183**: lú šu-bad a-hu-ti dub-sar, "men received by Ahuti, the scribe".

**184**: dumu-dumu šà-é-gal, "palace personnel"

**185**: 7 im-ru,"(they are) 7 administrative district/unit"

**186**: dumu-dumu ba?-DU, "personnel who have been assigned".

The officials in charge of the personnel listed in **181** are regularly identified by their profession. In **186**, besides the profession, the rank of ugula is sometimes indicated. In **182** and **184** the professional name follows the anthroponym only in some cases due to evident homonymy: šubur sagi, šubur muhaldim; NI.NI agrig, NI.NI sa-HAR. In the remaining texts, their names are not followed by any characterizing element.

Given the very close correspondences among the six texts, we can conclude that all the personnel listed in our documents belong to the administration of the é-gal and were probably employed for reasons of common interest. It should be noted that in the dumu-dumu texts the food allocated is flour and not barley as was the case in the other ration texts.

A comparison between the officials mentioned in these texts and those identified in the barley texts of the I group (in particular **2** and **3**) who, as we know, belong to the same centre as the é-gal enable us to reach the following conclusions.

The general summary text **1** lists four surviving items concerning the supply of monthly allocations of barley to four groups of dumu-dumu (cf. *Šuruppak*, pp.30, 34, 36-38). Now, two of these items correspond to the summaries of texts **2** and **3** which are each divided into six sections. Each of these sections groups the personnel of the palace administration who exercise the same profession under the responsibility of an ugula.

The texts which correspond to the two surviving items of **1** have not survived; but the primary documentation **9-13** mentions, as well as the twelve ugulas, fourteen others not named in **2** and **3**. These 14 ugulas recur as the persons in charge of the personnel who receive barley rations and they themselves are sometimes mentioned as the beneficiaries of rations. It is probable that the allocations to the dumu-dumu personnel of the primary tablets **9-13** were grouped in texts analogous to **2** and **3** which must have had correspondences to the other two dumu-dumu items of text **1**.

What follows is a list of the twenty six ugulas together with the profession for which they are responsible:

| PROFESSION | PERSONAL NAME |
|---|---|
| ugula-a-zu$_5$ : | lú-é-zi. |
| ugula-ad-KID: | dumu-nun-šita; é-nu-si. |
| ugula-agrig: | dub-hul-tar; NI.NI; šubur. |
| ugula-dilmun: | ur-nígin-si. |
| ugula-kínda: | lú-lum-ma. |
| ugula-lú-ad: | DI-utu[4] ; é-UD-nu-dib; $^{d}$sùd-ur-sag; ur-é-gal. |
| ugula-maškim: | é-ki-ba; har-tu-$^{d}$sùd. |
| ugula-muhaldim: | nin-unken-a; šubur. |
| ugula-munu$_4$: | KA-zi-da. |
| ugula-nar: | AK |
| ugula-sagi: | AN.URUDU-si; šubur. |
| ugula-sukkal: | é-nu-kur-si; lú-na-nam. |
| ugula-zadim: | é-ki-gal-la. |
| ugula-X: | amar-šùba. |
| ugula-X: | mes-ki-na. |
| ugula-X: | NI.NI. |

4 For the reading silim-utu cf. P.Steinkeller, *Observation on the Sumerian Personal Names in Ebla sources and on the Onomasticon of Mari and Kish*, in *The Tablet and the Scroll: Near Eastern Studies in Honor of William W. Hallo*, M.E.Cohen-D.C.Snell-D.B.Weisberg, Bethesda 1993, p.239.

These twenty six ugulas, with the exclusion of dumu-nun-šita ugula ad-KID, ur-nígin-si ugula dilmun and amar-šùba, are also the officials in charge of the dumu-dumu mentioned in the groups of texts regarding the personnel under examination. The correspondence is established by the identity of the professional name which follows each anthroponym; the term ugula is added once; in addition, this enables us to identify the profession of some of the ugulas, which in the texts of the first group was not documented; in particular, mes-ki-na is to be identified with the (ugula) lú-HAR (cf. **181** r. II 5-6) and NI.NI with (ugula) sa-HAR/nar (cf. **181** v. I 6-7; **182** r .II 6-7; **184** v. II 4-5).

From an inverse comparison, it has been possible to identify é-ki-gal-la, mentioned in **181** r. IV 2 and in **182** r. III 4 without any indication, with the (ugula)-zadim of the texts of the first group.

Moreover, some of the ugulas listed in our six texts are not mentioned in the corresponding barley texts of the I group. In relation to their professions, they are:

| PROFESSION | PERSONAL NAME |
|---|---|
| ugula-bahar$_4$: | é-kur-ra (**182** r. IV 4; **184** v. I 7-II 1). |
| (ugula-) íl/šitim : | A.HU.HA (**182** r. IV 1; **184** v. I 1-2). |
| ugula-lú-ad: | lugal-ezen (**182** r. II 2; **184** r. III 4). |
| ugula-lú-di: | dar-da (**182** r. III 1-2);<br>lugal-PA-du$_{10}$ (**181** v. I 4-5; **186** v. I 1-2). |
| ugula-lú-nab: | uru$_{18}$ (**182** r. IV 5-6; **184** v. II 2-3). |
| ugula-túg-du$_8$ : | AK-$^d$sùd (**182** r. III 6; **184** r. IV 4). |
| (ugula-)X: | ba-za$_7$ (**181** r. II 4). |
| ugula-X: | KA-$^d$sùd-da-zi (**182** r. III 5; **184** r. IV 3). |
| ugula-X: | lú-pà (**182** r. III 3; **184** r. IV 1). |
| ugula-X: | sag-nar$_x$ (**181** r. II 3). |
| ugula-X: | ur-$^d$nin-PA (**181** r. I 4; **183** r. I 3; **184** r. I 1-3) |

Of the first five officials not followed by a professional name, two of them, KA-$^d$sùd-da-zi and lú-pà, can be identified; the former with the ugula simug mentioned in a contract (cf. TSŠ X r. III 4-5) and the latter with the (ugula-)nagar in a barley text (cf. **14** v. III 14'-15'). For the remaining three, there are no elements which might enable us to identify the profession for which they were responsible.

So, we can deduce from the dumu-dumu texts the names of twelve other ugulas who can be added to the twenty six mentioned in the barley texts of the I group as employed in the service of the é-gal. It is possible that other ugulas, mentioned in different types of texts, could belong to the administration of the é-gal[5].

In all, therefore, about forty ugulas seem to have worked in the administration of the é-gal, each in charge of an administrative unit all of whose personnel carried out the same professional activity. The different ugulas who were in charge of the personnel who carried out the same activity were probably subordinates of a single corporation head as the following comparison shows: UR.UR ugula kínda in **115** v. III and UR.UR gal-kínda in **124** v. III 12-13[6].

The numerical consistency of the administrative unit under the responsibility of the ugula seems to have been about 20 persons, as can be deduced from the barley texts **2** and **3**; but, in actual fact, in the light of **185**, we must hold that the number was greater. **185** lists seven officials, ugulas of the é-gal, who were responsible for seven im-rus. This meaning of this term, as we discussed in the commentary on the text, is "district" or "family", but the fact that each im-ru employed personnel of the same profession and that the supervisor was an ugula who exercised that profession (cf. *supra*, p.23-24) suggests that in Fara the word could have taken on a wider meaning than simply administrative district or group. Thus, these im-ru's may have indicated the administrative units we are studying here. The numbers which precede the names of the ugulas, as can be deduced from the colophon, are the number of persons in service in each im-ru, at least at the moment of the compilation of the document. In order, these numbers are: 76, 72, 77, 67, 67, 65, 113. If we exclude the im-ru of the ugula lú-ad DI-utu, the last of the series, we can reasonably suppose that each of the forty or so im-ru must have had an average of 70 persons. If we also take into account the personnel mentioned in **2** and **3** who were subordinates of the ugulas, the number of persons in each section is about equal. This implies that the

---

5 This concerns $^{d}$sùd-á-mah ugula a-zu$_5$ (cf. **116** v. II 16-17), UR.UR ugula kínda (cf. **115** v. III 16-17) and utu-ur-sag ugula sukkal (cf. **116** r. II 20-21; **121** v. III 7'-8'; **124** v. I 1-2). To these should be added é-na ugula é-gal (cf. WF 35 v. I 5-6).

6 As has already been shown (cf. *Šuruppak*, pp. 63; 136), the sequence PN gal-Prof.N generally indicates that the PN is a subordinate of the gal-Prof.N.

total number of the im-ru's of the é-gal had a staff of between 2,500 and 3,000 individuals.

## §.2 The guruš texts

**A)** A second group of eight documents **(187-194)** concerning the guruš personnel features large-scale and reciprocal correlations with the texts we have already noted in regard to the dumu-dumu personnel. The analysis of these correlations enables us to identify some administrative and organizational structures both of the administrative centre of the é-gal and of that of the é-uru.

Both **196** and **195** should certainly be added to these documents. The former is a text of which only one fragment of the verso has survived; here the final summary is registered. The latter is a document which, although it has a small number of items in common with other texts, has features which are similar to them. Therefore, its compilation must have had the same scope.

Finally, it should be noted that some of the texts examined (**186**; **192**; **193**; **196**) came from the site XVII c,d, as did the dumu-dumu texts. In this case, too, one can reasonably suppose that the entire group came from the same site (cf. *infra*, p.84).

**187(WF 95)**

r. I 1) 60 guruš
2) é-na
3) ki-mu-$gi_4$
4) maš-$da_5$
5) ur-dumu-zi(1)
6) 60 AN-nume(2)
7) $bil_x$-kalam-$du_{10}$(3)

8) mes-é-[zi]-da(4)

II 1) 60 $al_6$-la
2) ur-$^d$sùd(5)
3) nam-mah(6)
4) é-gal
5) 60 ur-$^d$sùd(7)
6) nu-bànda$^{da}$
7) munus-geštin(8)
8) $bil_x$-anzu(9)
9) 60 maš-$da_5$(10)
10) $al_6$-lum(11)

III 1) é-na(12)
2) ŠEŠ-ki-na(13)
3) 60 AK-$^d$tu
4) sipa
5) nin-ur-sag(14)
6) ad-da(15)
7) sipa-anše
8) šà-uru
9) 60 $^d$sùd-anzu
10) ugula-kínda

IV 1) sag-TAR
2) $^d$sùd-anzu(16)
3) ur-é-nun-gal(17)
4) ur-$^d$sùd
5) maškim
6) lugal-ezen(18)
7) lùmgi
8) 60 kun-$du_6$(19)
9) KA-ni-zi(20)
10) sagi

| | | | |
|---|---|---|---|
| v. | I | 1) | munus-u$_4$-ba |
| | | 2) | muhaldim |
| | | 3) | 60 $^{d}$sùd-anzu |
| | | 4) | é-šùd-du$_{10}$ |
| | | 5) | dub-sar |
| | | 6) | nam-mah[21] |
| | | 7) | sipa |
| | | 8) | 60 AN-nu-me |
| | | 9) | é-géme |
| | | 10) | amar-$^{d}$gú-lá |
| | II | 1) | gal-nimgir[22] |
| | | 2) | KA-ni-zi |
| | | 3) | sa$_{12}$-du$_5$[23] |
| | | 4) | 60 GAR-da-nu-tuku[24] |
| | | 5) | amar-šùba[25] |
| | | 6) | simug |
| | | 7) | é-DÚR |
| | | 8) | šu-ku$_6$ |
| | | 9) | DI-utu[26] |
| | | 10) | sanga-GAR |
| | III | 1) | 20 lú-IGI.NÍGIN (LAK 431) |
| | | 2) | $^{d}$sùd-anzu |
| | | 3) | a-a |
| | IV | 1) | an-šè-gú |
| | | 2) | 680 guruš-mè |

(1) Cf. 12 (**188** r. IV 4).

(2) 2 (**192** r. I 1-2); 19 (**188** r. I 1-2).

(3) 3 (**192** r. I 3).

(4) 4 (**192** r. I 6); 9 (**189** v. I 3').

(5) 2 (**192** r. I 4); 3 (**189** v.I 4'); 14 (**188** r. I 3).
(6) 8 (**192** r. I 5); 9 (**189** v. I 2').
(7) 73 (**188** r. I 5).
(8) 12 (**188** r. I 4).
(9) 60 (**188** r. I 6).
(10) 1 (**192** r. II 5); cf. 3 maš-$da_5$ sagi (**189** v. II 3'-4').
(11) 6 (**192** r. II 6).
(12) 1 (**192** r. III 1); cf. é-na engar: 1 (**195** r. IV 13-V 1).
(13) 1 (**192** r. III 2).
(14) 10 (**188** r. III 6); cf. 1 nin-ur-sag IB (**195** r. VII 12-VIII 1).
(15) 12 (**192** r. III 5); 50 (**190** r. II 3).
(16) Cf. 7 (**189** v. III 3').
(17) Cf. 10 (**195** r. I 1).
(18) Cf. 6 lùmgi (**192** r. II 3).
(19) 10 (**189** v. II 1').
(20) 8 (**189** v. II 2').
(21) Cf. 11 nam-mah é-am-$du_7$ (**195** v. I 11-12); 19 sipa-énsi-GAR (**191** r. II 1'-2').
(22) Cf. 27 gal-nimgir (**188** r. III 2).
(23) Cf. 36 $sa_{12}$-$du_5$ (**188** r. III 3); KA-ni-zi ur-$^{d}$lamma (**195** r. VII 2-3).
(24) 23 (**188** r. III 4); [x+]14 (**191** r. I 3').
(25) Cf. 13 (**191** r. II 4'); 20 (**188** r. IV 1).
(26) Cf. 10 (**190** r. II 4); 4 (**192** r. IV 1).

The tablet is whole and has four columns both on the recto and verso. The 26 notes on the text indicate, in accordance with the method adopted in *Šuruppak*, the correspondences with the remaining nine texts. Most of them are certain; and, even though some are not certain (notes 17, 18, 22, 23) they are highly probable.

## 188 (CT 50, 1)

r I 1) 19 guruš
2) AN-nu-me(1)
3) 14 ur-$^{d}$sùd(2)

| | | |
|---|---|---|
| | 4) | 62 munus-geštin(3) |
| | 5) | 73 ur-$^{d}$sùd(4) |
| | 6) | 60 bil$_x$-anzu(5) |
| II | 1) | 61 mes-lu-lu(6) |
| | 2) | 70 dumu-$^{d}$anzu(7) |
| | 3) | 76 ad-da(8) |
| | 4) | 63 DI-utu(9) |
| | 5) | 25 nagar(10) |
| | 6) | 20 simug(11) |
| | 7) | 11 ašgab |
| | 8) | 3 nu-kiri$_6$(12) |
| III | 1) | 23 abgal(13) |
| | 2) | 27 gal-nimgir(14) |
| | 3) | 35 sa$_{12}$-du$_5$(15) |
| | 4) | 24 šita-da-nu-tuku(16) |
| | 5) | 15 é-su$_{13}$-ág |
| | 6) | 9 nin-ur-sag(17) |
| IV | 1) | 20 amar-šùba(18) |
| | 2) | 18 amar-tùr(19) |
| | 3) | 12 amar-nam-nir(20) |
| | 4) | 12 ur-dumu-zi(21) |
| | 5) | 60 enku(22) |
| v. I-II | | blank |
| v. III | 1) | blank |
| | 2) | šu-nígin 858 guruš |

(1) **187** r. I 6; 2 (**192** r. I 1-2).

(2) **187** r.II 2; 2 192 r. I 4); 3 (**189** v. I 3').

(3) **187** r. II 7.

(4) 60 ur-$^{d}$sùd nu-bànda (**187** r. II 5-6).

(5) **187** r. II 8.

(6) 5 (**192** r. III 5); 40 (**190** r. II 1).

(7) 5 (**192** r. III 6); 40 (**190** r. II 1).

(8) 12 (**192** r. III 7); 50 (**190** r. II 3). Cf. ad-da sipa-anše (**187** r. III 6-7).

(9) 4 (**192** r. III 8); 10 (**190** r. II 4).

(10) 19 (**191** r. I 6').

(12) 2 (**193** r. I 1); cf. 23 nu-kiri$_6$ sanga-GAR (**191** r. II 3'-4').

(13) 2 (**192** r. IV 4); 10 (**191** r. III 1').

(14) Cf. amar-$^{d}$gú-lá gal-nimgir (**187** v. I 10-II 1).

(15) 43 (**191** r. III 2')$^?$; cf. KA-ni-zi sa$_{12}$-du$_5$ (**187** v. II 2-3); KA-ni-zi ur-$^{d}$lamma (**195** r. VII 2-3).

(16) **187** v. II 4; [x+]14 (**191** r. II 5').

(17) **187** r. III 5. Cf. 1 nin-ur-sag IB (**195** r. VII 12-VIII 1)

(18) 12 (**191** r. II 5'); cf. amar-šùba simug (**187** v. II 5-6).

(19) 8 (**191** r. II 6').

(20) 8 (**191** r. II 7').

(21) Cf. **187** r. I 5.

(22) 1 (**195** v. I 1); 3 (**193** r. II 6); 8 (**192** v. I 1).

This tablet lists 22 items; with the exclusion of r. III 6, they all have correspondences with items in other texts. The anthroponymn GAR-da-nu-tuku mentioned in **191** r. II 5 must be considered a variant of šita-da-nu-tuku mentioned in r. III 4. The fact that the two signs are alike must have, on occasion, caused the scribes to commit errors in writing. The items, 27 gal-nimgir, 36 sa$_{12}$-du$_5$ in r. III 2-3 should be identified with the items in sequence in **187** v. I 10-II 3, amar-$^{d}$gú-lá gal-nimgir KA-ni-zi sa$_{12}$-du$_5$. The scribe of our text, perhaps only interested in the offices, that of the gal-nimgir and sa$_{12}$-du$_5$, the guruš came from, omitted in this case the personal names of the officials in charge.

## 189 (NTSŠ 114)

| | | | |
|---|---|---|---|
| v. | I | 1') | 3 [ur]-$^{d}$sùd(1) |
| | | 2') | 9 nam-mah(2) |
| | | 3') | 9 mes-é-zi-da(3) |
| | | 4') | 4 [ ] |
| | II | 1') | 10 kun-du$_6$(4) |
| | | 2') | 8 KA-ni-zi(5) |
| | | 3') | 3 maš-da$_5$(6) |
| | | 4') | sagi |
| | | 5') | 13 [ ] |
| | III | 1') | 4 eden-AŠ |
| | | 2) | 11 lú-HAR |
| | | 3') | 7 $^{d}$sùd-anzu(7) |
| | IV | 1') | [x+]134 še-ba |
| | | 2') | lú šu-ba-ti |

(1) **187** r. II 2; 2 (**192** r. I 4); 14 (**188** r. I 3).

(2) **187** r. II 3; 8 (**192** r. I 5).

(3) **187** r. I 8; 4 (**192** r. I 6).

(4) **187** r. IV 8.

(5) **187** r. IV 9-10; cf. 2 KA-ni-zi ur-$^{d}$lamma (**195** r. VII 2-3).

(6) 1 (**192** r. II 5); cf. (**187** r. II 9).

(7) Cf. **187** r. IV 2.

Only a large fragment of the verso of this text has survived. It has been identified as a guruš document because a large part of its items, often in order, correspond to analogous items in **187** and **192**.

## 190 (TSŠ 894)

r. I 1) 10 dumu-ama-bára-si
2) 10 ur-$^{d}$tu[(1)]
3) 10 dumu-nun-šita
4) ur-é-gal[(2)]
blank

II 1) 40 mes-lu-lu[(3)]
2) 50 dumu-anzu[(4)]
3) 50 ad-da[(5)]
4) 10 DI-utu[(6)]
5) 10 ur-$^{d}$gú-[lá[(7)]]

(1) Cf. 5 (**195** r. I 8).
(2) 1 (**195** r. V 7-8).
(3) 5 (**192** r. III 5); 61 (**188** r. II 1).
(4) 5 (**192** r. III 6); 70 (**188** r. II 2).
(5) 12 (**192** r. III 7); 76 (**188** r. II 3).
(6) 4 (**192** r. III 8); 63 (**188** r. II 4).
(7) Cf. 2 (**195** r. IV 5).

This small text, of which only the recto has survived, consists in two columns. It lists two groups, of three and five items respectively, each separated by an unwritten line. The single items do not indicate, however, what the meaning of the numbers preceding the anthroponyms is. The correspondences with **188**, **192**, **195** and **196** enable us to establish that this is a guruš text. The verso must have contained the colophon with the summary but a third group of items could also have been listed.

## 191 (TSŠ 783)

r. I 1') 5 maškim
2') šùš[1]
3') [x+]14 GAR-da-nu-tuku[2]
4') 9 AN-dùl-du$_{10}$
5') šitim
6') 19 nagar[3]
some lines destroyed

II 1') 19 sipa énsi$^{!}$(TE.SI)-GAR[4]
2') 13 maškim sanga-GAR[5]
3') 23 nu-kiri$_{6}$[6]
4') sanga GAR
5') 12 amar-šùba[7]
6') 8 amar-tùr[8]
7') 8 amar-[nam-n]ir[9]
some lines destroyed

III 1') 10 abgal[10]
2') 43 túl$^{?}$-sag[11 a] / sa$_{12}$-du$_{5}$$^{?}$[11 b]
3') 21 ur-$^{d}$nin-mú[12]
4') 10 šà-ezen[13]
5') 16 $^{d}$sùd-anzu[14]
6') 16 nimgir-teme-na
6') 16 mušen$^{?}$-dù
some lines destroyed

IV 1') 12[+x] [ ]
2') 19 a-[geš]tin$^{!}$[15]
3') 28 é-nu-si[16]
4') 24 šeš-[á]-nu-kúš[17]
5') 40 [ ]
some lines destroyed

v. I-IV destroyed

(1) 4 (**193** r. II 4-5).
(2) **187** v. II 4; 23 (**188** r. III 4).
(3) 25 (**188** r. II 4).
(4) Cf. nam-mah sipa (**187** v. I 6-7); 11 nam-mah é-am-du$_7$ (**195** v. I 11-12).
(5) 1 (**193** r. II 2-3).
(6) Cf. nu-kiri$_6$ **193** r. I 1; 3 (**188** r. II 8).
(7) 20 (**188** r. IV 1).
(8) 18 (**188** r. IV 2).
(9) 12 (**188** r. IV 3).
(10) 2 (**192** r. IV 4); 23 (**188** r. III 1).
(11a) 2 ur-túl-sag (**192** v. I 2).
(11b) 36 (**188** r. III 3); cf. KA-ni-zi sa$_{12}$-du$_5$ (**187** v. II 2-3).
(12) 2 (**194** r. I 1-2).
(13) 2 (**194** r. I 3).
(14) 2 (**194** r. I 4).
(15) 19 (**193** r. III 1).
(16) 3 (**193** r. III 2).
(17) 4 (**193** r. III 3).

This tablet has several lacunae; only the recto has survived but its upper left-hand part has been abrased. As in the case of **188** and **190**, the typology of this document has been identified only by the correspondences between it and other texts of the group. 18 of the 19 surviving items are related to all the other texts; and it is possible that the nineteenth item in r. III 6' corresponds to the fourth in **194**[7] .

TSŠ in r. III 2' copies UDU-sag, an anthroponym never mentioned elsewhere. This should be read túl-sag which should be regarded as an abbreviation of ur-túl-sag mentioned in **192** (note 11a). But the reading sa$_{12}$-du$_5$ is also possible; this is a

7 One cannot exclude that the sign copied in TSŠ as mušen is a part of the sign ùsan. In actual fact, our text has a sequence of three items (r. III 3'-5') in common with **194** r. I 1-4 and the fourth item of **194** mentions šubur ùsan-dù which could correspond to the item in our text.

professional name which could indicate the office from which the guruš came. It has a correspondence in **187** and **188** (note 11b).

TSŠ in r. IV 2' copies a-ru but the comparison with the sequence in common with **193** r. III 1-3 suggests reading a-geštin.

## 192 (WF 98)

r. I 1) 2 guruš
2) AN.mu-me(1)
3) 3 $bil_x$-kalam-$du_{10}$(2)
4) 2 ur-$^{d}$sùd(3)
5) 8 nam-mah(4)

II 1) 4 mes-é-zi-da(5)
2) 1 sukkal
3) 1 muhaldim
4) 6 lùmgi(6)
5) 1 [m]aš-d[$a_5^?$](7)
6) 6 a[$l_6$]-lum(8)

III 1) 1 é-na(9)
2) 1 ŠEŠ-ki-na(10)
3) 5 mes-lu-lu(11)
4) 5 dumu-anzu(12)
5) 12 ad-da(13)

IV 1) 4 DI-utu(14)
2) 2 utu-ur-sag
3) 2 $azlag_4$
4) 4 [AL]AM
5) 2 abgal(15)

v. I 1) 8 enk[u](16)

2) 2 túl-sag-[d]$u_{10}$[(17)]

blank

II blank

III 1) an-šè-gú 82 guruš

2) 2 (bàn) zì šu-ba-ti

3) 27 gurxU (bariga) 2 (bàn)

4) lú zì-ba

(1) **187** r. I 6; 19 (**188** r. I 1-2).
(2) **187** r. I 7.
(3) **187** r. II 2; 14 (**188** r. I 3); 3 (**189** v. I 1').
(4) **187** r. II 3; 9 (**189** v. I 2').
(5) **187** r. I 8; 9 (**189** v. I 3').
(6) Cf. lugal-ezen lùmgi (**187** r. IV 5-6).
(7) **187** r. II 9.
(8) **187** r. II 10.
(9) **187** r. III 1.
(10) **187** r. III 2.
(11) 40 (**190** r. II 1); 61 (**188** r. II 1).
(12) 40 (**190** r. II 2); 70 (**188** r. II 2).
(13) 50 (**190** r. II 3); 76 (**188** r. II 3).
(14) 10 (**190** r. II 4); 63 (**188** r. II 4).
(15) 10 (**191** r. III 1').
(16) 1? (**195** v. I 1); 3 (**193** r. II 6); 60 (**188** r. IV 5).
(17) Cf. 43 túl?-sag (**191** r. III 2').

This text, with four written columns on the recto and two on the verso, lists 21 items. Of these, 17 are related to items in other texts in this group. The flour allocated to the guruš is measured in gur of one bariga as indicated in the colophon. This unit of dry measurement could be regarded as a graphical variant of the sign for the bariga mentioned in the documentation of Fara in only one other text (cf. G.Visicato, *Unità di misura di capacità a Fara: bariga e gur-mah*, NABU 1991, p.54, note 3). The sequence r. II 6-III 2 parallel to **187** r. II 9-III 2 has enabled us to integrate the anthroponym maš-$da_5$ in r. II 5.

### 193 (WF 102)

r. I 1) 2 nu-$kiri_6$[(1)]
2) 2 maškim
3) 2 dub-sar
4) $sa_{12}$-$du_5$
5) 2 maškim

II 1) dub-sar
2) 1 maškim
3) sanga-GAR[(2)]
4) 4 maškim
5) šùš[(3)]
6) 3 enku[(4)]

III 1) 19 a-geštin[(5)]
2) 3 é-nu-si[(6)]
3) 4 šeš-á-nu-kúš[(7)]

v. I-II blank/destroyed

III 1) [an-šè-gú] 20[+x] [guruš]
2) [ ]

(1) 3 (**188** r. II 7); cf. 23 nu-$kiri_6$ sanga-GAR (**191** r. II 3'-4').

(2) 13 (**191** r. II 2').

(3) 5 (**191** r. I 1').

(4) 1[?] (**195** v. I 1); 8 (**192** v. I 1); 60 (**188** r. IV 5).

(5) 19 (**191** r. IV 2').

(6) 28 (**191** r. IV 3').

(7) 24 (**191** r.IV 4').

**193** is a small text which lists 10 items on the recto, six of which are related to **191**. The verso contains the colophon of which only some numerals are legible.

## 194 (TSŠ 249)

r. I 1) 2 guruš
2) ur-$^{d}$nin-mú(1)
3) 2 šà-ezen(2)
4) 2 $^{d}$sùd-anzu(3)
5) [ ].TI$^{?}$.SAR$^{?}$

II 1) 2 šubur
2) ùsan-dù(4)
3) enku
4) blank

(1) 21 (**191** r. III 3').
(2) 10 (**191** r. III 4').
(3) 16 (**191** r. III 5').
(4) Cf. 16 (**191** r. III 6')$^{?}$.

This is the smallest text in the group and contains only four surviving items, all of which are probably related to **191**. It is probable that this text mentions officials who belonged to the same office. This could be identified with that of the enku since this official is mentioned at the end of the text. It is unclear whether the surviving signs in r. I 5 indicate the name of a profession or an anthropnym; as far as we are aware, an anthroponym partly constituted of the signs TI and SAR seems nowhere to be found in the onomasticon of Fara. One cannot exclude the possibility that TSŠ had not copied the sign faithfully; in fact, from a comparison with the sequence in **191** r. IV 3'-7' and that in TSŠ 969 (cf *infra*, p.58-59) one would expect the mention of the anthroponym nimgir-teme-na.

## 195 (WF 100)

r. I 1) 10 guruš
2) ur-é-nun-gal[1]
3) 3 šubur
4) abzu-⌜ki⌝-⌜du$_{10}$⌝
5) 2 $^{d}$s[ùd]-⌜á⌝-mah
6) 1 amar-⌜abzu⌝
7) UR.UR
8) 5 KA-lugal-da-zi
9) 5 ur-$^{d}$tu[2]

II 1) 3 amar-šùba
2) a-ki-[ga]l
3) 3 ur-é-nun-gal
4) mu$_{6}$-sùb
5) 3 lum-ma
6) abgal
7) 3 AN-nu-me
8) maš-$^{d}$sùd
9) 5 har-tu-$^{d}$sùd
10) gi$_{4}$-za$_{7}$

III 1) 2 nam-mah
2) šeš-tur
3) 2 amar-šùba
4) da[m-gà]r
5) 2 [l]am-[ma]
6) abzu-ki-du$_{10}$
7) 2 sag-nar$_{x}$ [en]gar
8) 1 maš-lugal
9) 5 é-tigi$_{x}$
10) 5 ŠIR$^{?}$-MUNU$_{4}^{?}$
11) 5 AN-nu-me

12) é-sahar-ta-è

IV 1) 3 AN-nu-me
2) gal-nimgir
3) 1 amar-$^{d}$gú-lá
4) šùš
5) 2 ur-$^{d}$gú-lá(3)
6) 2 mes-$u_4$-b[a] abgal
7) 6 $pa_4$-alim
8) 6 sag-$nar_x$
9) eden-s[i]
10) 2 amar-abzu
11) engar
12) 1 é-na

V 1) engar
2) 2 har-tu-$^{d}$sùd
3) a-$du_7$
4) 2 é-na-lu-lu
5) lú-$^{giš}$BÙLUG
6) 2 zà/é$^{?}$-ušum-gal
7) 1 dumu-nun-šita
8) ur-é-gal(4)
9) 1 a-NE-nu
10) 1 AN-nu-me
11) abzu-ki-$du_{10}$(5)
12) 1 a-hu-ti
13) dub-sar

VI 1) 2 dumu-nun-šita
2) a-$si_4$
3) 1 uš-dù
4) enku
5) 1 GAR-ur-sag

6) dam-gàr
7) 2 NI.NI
8) ama-bur-e
9) 2 [l]ú-lum-[ma]
10) LAK 60-ma
11) 1 AK.AN
12) mar
13) 2 lum-ma
14) $pa_4$-anzu

VII 1) 2 en-[en]gar-zi
2) 2 KA-ni-zi
3) ur-$^{d}$lamma[(6)]
4) 1 ad-da
5) engar[(7)]
6) 1 $MUNU_4^{?}$.LA.X
7) 2 lú-géme-zi-d[a]
8) 1 a-<da>-DÚR
9) ur-$^{d}$gú-lá
10) 1 $^{d}$sùd-ur-sag
11) munus-á-nu-kúš
12) 1 nin-ur-sag

VIII 1) IB
2) 1 $pa_4$-á-nu-kúš
3) KA-n[un]-zi
4) 2 KA-zi$^{!}$
5) 1 še[š]-n[i]
6) munus-en-kalam
7) 1 lu-lu
8) šubur
9) 1 me-pa-è
10) engar
11) 1 AN-nu-me

12) lugal-KA-zu

13) 1 [ ]-hur-sag

v. I 1) 1 a-n[un]-p[á]

2) enku

3) 1 ama-gal$^{?}$-gal

4) 1 é-hur-sag

5) 1 $^{d}$sùd-ur-sag

6) maš-$^{d}$sùd

7) 1 AK

8) munu$_4$

9) 1 lu-lu

10) MI

11) 1 nam-mah

12) é-am-du$_7$(8)

13) 1 nin-anzu

II 1) IB

2) 1 nin-ul$_4$-gal

3) IB

4) 1 gúr-gúr

5) sa$_{12}$-du$_5$

blank

III blank

IV 1) an-šè-gú

2) 142 šubur

3) *bur-šu-ma*

(1) Cf. **187** r. IV 3.

(2) 10 (**190** r. I 2).

(3) Cf. 10 (**190** r. II 5).

(4) 10 (**191** r. I 3-4.

(5) Cf. AN-nu-me é-géme (**187** v. I 8-9).

(6) Cf. KA-ni-zi $sa_{12}$-$du_5$ (**187** v. II 2-3); 36 $sa_{12}$-$du_5$ (**188** r. III 3).

(7) Cf. 76 (**188** r. II 3); 50 (**190** r. II 3).

(8) Cf. nam-mah sipa (**187** v. I 6-7).

This long text is intact apart from some abrasions. It contains eight written columns on the recto and three on the verso. The second column on the verso which concludes the list of items has only five written lines; the rest is unwritten. The colophon which gives the total number of guruš recruited under the responsibility of šubur *bur-šu-ma*, "the senior Šubur", is placed on the extreme right of the tablet, as was customary in the Fara texts.

The integration in r. III 5 of [la]m-[ma] was suggested by the presence of the characterizing element, the anthroponym abzu-ki-$du_{10}$. lam-ma abzu-ki-$du_{10}$ is mentioned in the texts concerning fields and carts (cf. **68** r. II 9-10; **69** v. II 7-8; **172** r. V 1'-2'). We proceeded in a similar way for a-<da>-DÚR ur-[d]gú-lá (cf. **68** r. IV 9-10; **70** r. III 4-5; **74** r. III 4-5; **132** v. VI 5-6; **136** v. II 11-12; **142** r. IV 7-8) and [a]-nun-p[à] enku (cf. **121** r. VI 7-8; **122** r. V 4'-5'; **127** v. II 6-7; **132** r. VI 5-6; **153** r. III 3-4).

Of the 65 anthroponyms mentioned, only 8 have correspondences with the other texts of the group; but it should be noted that the great majority of them are mentioned in the texts concerning fields, asses and carts. This suggests that the guruš listed in this text were recruited from among the personnel assigned to agricultural work in the parcels of land granted to the various officials. Now, in **41**, one of the barley documents of the III group (cf. *Šuruppak*, p.182), two items are listed, one of 1560 gur and the other of 46 gur. The possible destination of the 1560 gur of the first item will be discussed later (cf. *infra*, p.85, note 30). To understand the destination of the 46 gur of the second item, we should recall that item is followed by the term *bur-šu-ma*[8] , considered to be the Semitic equivalent of the Sumerian libir (cf. *Šuruppak*, p.179). In fact, it cannot be excluded that it indicates, by mentioning just the professional name, the šubur *bur-šu-ma* mentioned in our text as the person in charge of the 142 guruš recruited from among the personnel assigned to the $aša_5$-šuku. In

---

8 For a mention of the profession *bur-šu-ma*, "the senior" in the Old-Akk. period cf.. A.Westenholz, OSP 2, p. 121, **100** v. I 6'-7': ur-[d]inanna lú *bur-su-ma*.

that case, the 46 gur in question could have been destined for the sustenance of those personnel. With regard to the identity of the "senior" šubur, we should recall that many of the recruitment texts mention in the colophon the dub-sar in charge of the enlisted men (cf. *infra*, p.85). It is, therefore, possible that this official could be identified with the ugula dub-sar mentioned in **116** r.V 11-12 and described as dub-sar sanga-GAR in TSŠ 430 r. III' 4'-5'.

**196 (WF 97)**

v. I' 1') šu-nígin 6580 guruš

Only a small fragment of this document has survived; and only the verso containing the colophon is legible. Judging from the form of the fragment, this tablet must have been small. Given the large number of guruš mentioned in the šu-nígin, it must be regarded as a summary referring perhaps to a previous phase of compilation respect of the other texts.

**B)** As can be observed from the notes on the texts, the compilation technique of the documents examined, with the differences we have already noted in the case of the dumu-dumu texts, is substantially similar to that of the texts concerning the allocation of goods. Among these documents the following types can be identified: general summaries, partial summaries, intermediate texts and primary texts.

1) GENERAL SUMMARIES: **196**.

**196** appears as a general summary of guruš texts. It may be, given its reduced size, a similar texte to 1, the general summary of barley texts og I group (cf, Šururppak, p.88; 35). Thus it is probable that on the recto, completely lost, the guruš were divided into a smaller number of groups in reference to the centres or the cities whence they came.

2) PARTIAL SUMMARIES: **187**, **188**.

With the exclusion of **193** and **194**, **187** has correspondences with all the other texts. In some cases, entire sequences (which will be examined in detail) of our text are repeated in other documents of the group, though with different numbers. However, several items have no correspondences. This means that the summary text **187** also groups the items present in other intermediate or primary texts which have not survived. Similarly, just over 20 items of other texts find no correspondences in **187**. Of these, about 10 have correspondences with **188**, the other partial summary text.

There is a particular relationship between **187** and **188**. The latter text has fewer items than the former; but in the corresponding items, the number of guruš which precedes the anthroponym in **188** is higher than that recorded in **187**. Thus the relationship would appear to be similar to that of **183** and **184**, already encountered in the analysis of the dumu-dumu texts; and it is therefore likely that the compilation of **188** followed that of **187**. Apart from the large number of correspondences with **187**, **188** is related to all the other texts with the exception of **194**. From what has been said, we must conclude that **187** and **188** cannot contain all the documents of the partial summary. At least one other text of this type must have grouped both the items which have found no correspondences in **187** and **188** and the items in **195**.

3) INTERMEDIATE TEXTS: **189, 190, 191**.

All the items of **189**, with one exception, have correspondences in **187**; some of them have also correspondences with **188** and **192**.

**190** lists eight items divided into two sections; the items of the first section correspond to **195** while four of the items in sequence in the second section correspond both with **188** and the primary text **192**. The total number of the guruš recruited in **191** is less than in the corresponding items of **188** and greater than those in **192**. This demonstrates that the compilation of **191** should certainly be placed chronologically between these two texts.

**191** has 19 surviving items. Of these, five (notes 2, 8, 9, 10, 12b) have correspondences only with the partial summary texts, seven (notes 1, 6, 13, 14, 15, 16, 17) only with the two primary texts **193** and **194**. The remaining items display correspondences both with the primary texts and the summary texts; but they have no item in common with the other intermediate texts **189** and **190**.

4) PRIMARY TEXTS: **192**, **193**, **194**.

We have considered **192** and **193** to be primary texts which should not have any items in common in spite of the fact that there is one item in **192** (v. I 1) which corresponds to another in **193** (r. II 6) and this is the only exception among the 31 items listed in the two texts.

**192** is a list of 21 items which correspond to all the other texts of the group. The sequences in common with **187**, **188**, **189** (notes 2, 4, 5) and with **187** and **190** (notes 11-14) are particularly interesting. We shall discuss the relationship between this text and **195** in the paragraphs which follow.

**193** lists 10 items. Besides the particular correspondence with **191**, it has two items in correspondence with **188** but none with **187**.

**194** lists 4 surviving items and a few signs of a fifth. The first three correspond to the sequence of three items in **191** (r. III 3'-5'). One cannot exclude that the fourth item, only partially legible, could correspond to the item in **191** r. IV 6'. As was pointed out in the commentary on **191**, it is possible that the fifth item, šubur ùsan-dù enku, could correspond to the item that follows the four items in sequence in **191** (r. III 7').

**195** is a particular case. Because of the number of its items this texts should be linked to the partial summary documents; however, because of the very modest numbers of guruš mentioned in the individual items, it should be linked to the primary texts. Since the text has correspondences with the other texts of the group, that is, four with **187** (notes 1, 6, 8; 10), three with **190** (notes 2, 3; 7), two with **188** (6; 7) and one with **191** (notes 4), we must accept that the scope of this document was the same as the others of this group with one difference, probably to be attributed to the officials who recruited the guruš. These officials, as was shown in the commentary on the text, were, for the most part, beneficiaries of parcels of land. It is possible that the items in correspondence indicate officials who had recruited the guruš who worked in the fields previously allocated to these officials by the administration for their sustenance as well as the guruš who worked under them on behalf of the administration. It is likely that these latter guruš were registered in the summary documents together with the former.

**192** is a document analogous to **195**, even though it lists a smaller number of items. In fact, a large number of the 21 anthroponyms and professional names mentioned in this text are identifiable with certainty as officials who were beneficiaries of parcels of land. Besides, the number of guruš recruited in the individual items is the same as that recorded in **195**. Finally, it should be noted that, with a single exception, **192** has no correspondences with **195**. Consequently, it is probable that **192** and **195** were documents written in sequence and that they registered the recruitment only of those guruš assigned to work in the aša$_5$-šuku.

**C) 187** lists 11 groups of officials each made up of three or four components; each group makes 60 guruš-mè available. To these 11 groups, a twelfth group, composed of only one official who supplies 20 men, should be added (cf. *Šuruppak*, p.12, note 13). The contribution of the individual officials within each group is not specified. From the concordances, it can be observed that many of these officials occur in other texts of this group in the same order in which they are listed in **187**. Differently from **187**, the number of men supplied by each official is specified in all the other texts.

What follows is a list of the sequences in common between **187** and the other texts in the group:

| **187** | **188** | **192** | **189** |
|---|---|---|---|
| r. I 6-II 8 | r. I 1-6 | r. I 1-II 1 | v. I 1'-2' |
| | 19 guruš | 2 guruš | [ ] |
| 60 AN-nu-me | AN-nu-me | AN.nu.me | [ ] |
| bil$_x$-kalam-du$_{10}$ | | 3 bil$_x$-kalam-du$_{10}$ | [ ] |
| mes-é-zi-da | | 4 mes-é-zi-da[ ] | |
| 60 al$_6$-la | | | |
| ur-$^d$sùd | 14 ur-$^d$sùd | 2 ur-$^d$sùd | 3 ur-$^d$sùd |
| nam-mah é-gal | | 8 nam-mah | 9 nam-mah |
| 60 ur-$^d$sùd | 73 ur-$^d$sùd | | |
| nu-bànda | | | |
| munus-geštin | 62 munus-geštin | | |
| bil$_x$-anzu | 60 bil$_x$-anzu | | |

| | | | |
|---|---|---|---|
| r. II 9-III 2 | | r. II 5-III 2 | |
| 60 maš-da$_5$ | | 1 ma[š]-da$_5$ | |
| al$_6$-lum | | 6 al$_6$-lum | |
| é-na | | 1 é-na | |
| ŠEŠ.KI-na | | 1 ŠEŠ.KI-na | |
| r. IV 8-10 | | | v. II 1'-4' |
| 60 kun-du$_6$ | | | 10 kun-du$_6$ |
| KA-ni-zi | | | 8 KA-ni-zi |
| | | | 3 maš-da$_5$ |
| sagi | | | sagi |
| v. I 8-II 6 | r. III 2-IV 1 | | |
| 60 AN-nu-me | | | |
| é-géme | | | |
| amar-$^{d}$gú-lá | | | |
| gal-nimgir | 27 gal-nimgir | | |
| KA-ni-zi | | | |
| sa$_{12}$-du$_5$ | 35 sa$_{12}$-du$_5$ | | |
| 60 GAR-da-nu-tuku | 24 šita-da-nu-tuku | | |
| amar-šùba | 20 amar-šùba | | |
| simug | | | |

Besides sequences in common with **187**, some texts in the group have sequences in common with other texts:

| **188** | **190** | **192** | **191** | **194** |
|---|---|---|---|---|
| r. II 1-4 | r. II 1-4 | r. III 5-8 | | |
| 61 mes-lu-lu | 40 mes-lu-lu | 5 mes-lu-lu | | |
| 70 dumu-$^{d}$anzu | 50 dumu-$^{d}$anzu | 5 dumu-$^{d}$anzu | | |
| 76 ad-da | 50 ad-da | 12 ad-da | | |
| 63 DI-utu | 10 DI-utu | 4 DI-utu | | |
| r. IV 1-3 | | | r. II 5'-7' | |
| 20 amar-šùba | | | 12 amar-šùba | |

| | | | |
|---|---|---|---|
| 18 amar-tùr | | 8 amar-tùr | |
| 12 amar-nam-nir | | 2 amar-nam-nir | |
| | | r. III 3'-5' | r. I 1-4 |
| | | 21 ur-$^{d}$nin-mú | 2 ur-$^{d}$nin-mú |
| | | 10 šà-ezen | 2 šà-ezen |
| | | 16 $^{d}$sùd-anzu | 2 $^{d}$sùd-anzu |

| **191** | **193** |
|---|---|
| r. IV 2'-4' | r. III 1-3 |
| 19 a-geštin | 19 a-geštin |
| 28 é-nu-si | 3 é-nu-si |
| 24 šeš-á-nu-kúš | 4 šeš-á-nu-kúš |

The method of compilation of the documents examined, the sequences they have in common and all the series of interconnected correspondences demonstrate without any doubt that the documents in question (**184-195**) must refer to various stages of the same operation.

Now, all the texts, with the exception of **194** which lists only 4 items without any notation[9] and **190** and **191** whose verso has not survived, contain a summary of the guruš in the colophon. Four of the eight texts which have a summary record an notation added after it.

**187**: guruš-mè, "personnel (recruited) for battle".
**189**: še-ba lú šu-ba-ti, "the men who have received their ration of barley".
**192**: 2 (bàn) zì šu-ba-ti 27 gurxU 2 (bàn) lú zì-ba, "the men who received 2 bàn of flour (for a total of) 27 bariga and 2 bàn, as rations"[10].

---

9 TSŠ copied only the recto of the tablet. Since the last line is unwritten it is probable that the verso was also unwritten. But it cannot be excluded that it contained the summary of the guruš listed on the recto.

10 The formula is substantially identical to that of **182** v. IV 1-4 but in this latter text the ration of flour allocated to each guruš was of 5 sìla while here it is 2 bàn which is equal to

**195**: šubur *bur-šu-ma*, "the senior Šubur (is in charge of the enlisted men)"

These added notations give us some insight into the nature of the operation in question. It must have consisted in the recruitment of about a thousand, or perhaps more, men who had to be maintained for warfare. The general summaries were, therefore, the final stage of the operation, that is, the total number of the men called up for military service; the partial summaries were the registers where the numbers of men from the different sectors were gradually totalized and the primary texts, which must have been the large majority, must have recorded on each occasion the drafting of men from the different sectors.

**D)** The provenance of workers from various sectors of the administration provides interesting elements for the identification of some administrative centres and some sectors of the economic activity of Šuruppak as well as indicating the stages of the conscription of soldiers. With this in mind, we shall analyse fifteen groups of officials who were in charge of the guruš. These are the eleven which follow one another in sequence in **187**, some of which are mentioned in the same order in other texts of the group, and the four identified from the sequences which are in common with other guruš texts but absent from **187**.

1) The first group (r. I 1-5) lists four officials: é-na, ki-mu-gi$_4$, maš-da$_5$ and ur-dumu-zi. The first three are mentioned as ugulas; some of the beneficiaries of the allocations of barley in the sequence in **23** (r. IV 10-V 3) are their subordinates. In the same text (r. III 8; v. I 12 and II 10) three lú-má are mentioned who are subordinates of ur-dumu-zi, the fourth official. Also in a text of LAHTANxGÚ (cf. BIN 8, 384 r. II 7-III 1 and IV 4'-5'), ki-mu-gi$_4$ and maš-da$_5$ are mentioned as addir$_x$ while ur-dumu-zi recurs as lú-má-gi$_6$ má-DÙN both in TSŠ 424 v. I 1-3, a SI.NUxŠUŠ text, and in the barley text **36** r. III 13-14.
   It is probable that the four officials were in charge of and controlled an administrative unit which employed personnel connected with boats.

---

20 sìla. It is probable that in the case of **182** there a weekly allocation was registered while in **192** this allocation was monthly.

2) The second group (r. I 6-8) lists three officials: AN-nu-me, $bil_x$-kalam-$du_{10}$ and mes-é-zi-da. These three officials are all ugulas mentioned in the barley texts of the II group. In fact, AN-nu-me is mentioned as ugula in **14** r. IV 24; VI 14-15; VII 2-3 and in the parallel texts **15-18**; he is mentioned as ugula-KISAL in **19** r. IV 16. $Bil_x$-kalam-$du_{10}$ is mentioned as ugula-KISAL in **14** r. V 5-6; VI 3-4; VII 14; 22-23; **28** r. IV 8-9; **29** r. III 14; WF 63 r. IV 1-2. mes-é-zi-da as ugula recurs in **14** v. II 17'-18'; **19** r. VIII 9-10; **23** v. I 13-14. The latter is also mentioned in a text concerning anše (**115** r. VII 2-3), in one concerning the allocation of textiles (BIN 8, 384 r. III 6) and in a text concerning personnel (**212** v. II' 1'). The fact that he is mentioned in **23** v. I 13-14 leads us to suppose that he is an ugula-lú-má.
On the basis of these attestations it is possible that the three anthroponyms mentioned are to be identified as officials of the KISAL, that is, engaged in the supervision of the personnel connected with boats.

3) The third group (r. II 1-4) lists $al_6$-la, ur-$^d$sùd and nam-mah é-gal. It is probable that at least two of these three officials, $al_6$-la and nam-mah (not mentioned elsewhere with the characterizing element é-gal[11] ), are to be identified with ugulas of the same name mentioned in connection with the lú-má personnel in the barley texts of the II group; the former is mentioned in **16** r. IV 8-9;12 and the latter in **14** r. I 8; 10-11; 19-20; II 15 and **29** r. I 4. The identification of ur-$^d$sùd appears to be more complex; however, he could be identified with the lú-má who comes from a place called ùru and who was a subordinate of amar-nam-nir ugula énsi-GAR.

4) The fourth group (r. II 5-8) lists the following: ur-$^d$sùd nu-bànda, munus-geštin and $bil_x$-$^d$anzu. ur-$^d$sùd nu-bànda must have been an official who was different from another official of the same name mentioned in the preceding group. Now, two officials with such an anthroponym are also mentioned in

11 The characterizing element which accompanies this anthroponym in our text probably served to distinguish this person from a šà-uru official of the same name (cf. CT 50, 5 v. II 1-3).

**23**, a document concerning barley rations to the lú-má; the first mentioned is a lú-má, a beneficiary of barley rations and a subordinate of the amar-nam-nir ugula of the énsi-GAR (cf. **23** r. VI 9-13 and the parallel passages of **24** r. V 14-VI 1 and **25** r. V 10-13). He is also mentioned in **26** r. IV 3-6, ur-$^{d}$sùd lú-má ùru amar-nam-ni-ir ugula and also in **18** v. IV 12-14 and **51** v. I 1-3). munus-geštin is an ugula, a subordinate of $^{d}$en-líl-pà to whom the lú-má who are beneficiaries of barley are subordinates (**23** r. III 2 and the parallel passages in **24** r. II 13 and **25** r. II 13-14; **23** r. VII 3-5 and the parallel passages in **24** r. V 15-VI 1 and **25** r. V 11-14). munus-geštin is also mentioned, but only as ugula, in **19** r. II 1; **29** r. IV 8 and as ugula-guruš in a texts concerning fibres, TSŠ 368 r. II 1-2. Now, in **23** r. II 10-III 2 the sequence of a group of subordinates who receive barley is mentioned. These workers, probably lú-má, are the subordinates of four ugulas in the order munus-geštin, ur-$^{d}$sùd, en-eden-si and $bil_x$-anzu. We can probably suppose that these four ugulas belonged to a single office. The following two considerations should be bourne in mind: firstly, that the names of the three officials mentioned in this fourth group, with the exception of en-eden-si, are the same as those of the ugulas mentioned in **23** r. II 10-III 2 and secondly, <en>-eden-si is mentioned in **23** v. IV 2-3 as a subordinate of nu-bànda while in the parallel passages (**24** r. VIII 11 and **25** v. I 1) he is mentioned as an ugula.

So, we can suppose that ur-$^{d}$sùd nu-bànda is to be identified as the ugula, the subordinate of $^{d}$en-líl-pà; in the same way, $bil_x$-anzu, en-eden-si and munus-geštin can be identified. Consequently, ur-$^{d}$sùd who is mentioned in the third group should be identified with the lú-má, the subordinate of amar-nam-nir. In addition, it should be noted that both munus-geštin and $bil_x$-$^{d}$anzu are mentioned as ugula-KISAL, the former in BIN 8, 384 r. I 1-2 and the latter in **132** r. VII 4-5 and **141** r. II 1-2. We can, therefore, reasonably conclude that the officials mentioned in the fourth group are ugulas working for the central office of the KISAL like those of the second group. The nu-bànda seems to have been the head of this centre and he should probably be identified with Enlil-pà (cf. *infra*, p.113-114).

5) The fifth group, r. II 9-III 2, lists four officials: é-na, $al_6$-lum, maš-$da_5$ and ŠEŠ-KI-na. $al_6$-lum is mentioned in **115** v. III 10-11 as an ugula-KISAL; maš-$da_5$ is mentioned in BIN 8, 384 r. IV 3 as $addir_x$ and ŠEŠ-KI-na as lú-má-$gur_8$ in **21** v. VI 3'-4'. It would seem possible that not only $al_6$-lum but also the latter two officials belonged to the administration of the KISAL since they were connected with boats. So, it is probable that even é-na, the first mentioned official, is connected with the same office. But in that case, if one does not wish to admit that the two officials, who have the same name and are not distinguished by a different characterizing element, carried out the same activity, é-na could be the ugula mentioned in the first group. The meaning of his mention in both groups escapes us.

6) The sixth group (r. III 3-8) lists: AK-$^{d}$tu sipa, nin-ur-sag and ad-da sipa-anše. AK-$^{d}$tu is not mentioned elsewhere with that qualification. nin-ur-sag should be identified with IB mentioned in **29** v. VI 5; **146** r. I 2-3; **165** r. III 1-2; there is a particular link between the IB officials and the cattle breeding centres (cf. *infra*, p.121, note 86). This official is described in NTSŠ 262 r. II 7-8 as IB gal-nimgir. ad-da sipa-anše šà-uru should be identified with the homonymous utul mentioned in **19** v. V 1-2; **31** r. III 1 and NTSŠ 262 r. I 3. In this case the presence of the second characterizing element, šà-uru, must have been necessary to distinguish this official from another of the same name who was probably in the employ of the é-gal. The mention in the same text, NTSŠ 262, a document concerning the allocation of goats, of two or three officials listed in this group, confirms the relationship which, on the basis of our text, seems to have existed between them.

7) The seventh group (r. III 9-IV 7) mentions six officials: $^{d}$sùd-anzu ugula kínda, sag-TAR, $^{d}$sùd-anzu, ur-é-nun-gal, ur-$^{d}$sùd maškim, lugal-ezen lùmgi. $^{d}$sùd-anzu, described in our text as ugula kínda, is nowhere else described in this way. sag-TAR is mentioned in **3** r. IV 5 as one of the maškim in the employ of é-ki-ba ugula-maškim; in TSŠ 614 r. I 4-6, a text concerning the allocation of different types of bread, sag-TAR has a maškim as his

subordinate and he himself is a subordinate of the sanga-GAR[12] . $^{d}$sùd-anzu is a maškim mentioned in BIN 8, 384 r. II 3 and in WF 138 v. I 1-2; the latter text which mentions the allocation of different types of goods to some officials could come from the site XVII c,d. ur-$^{d}$sùd maškim is mentioned in one of the primary texts of the I group of barley texts, **10** r. IV 4-5; he is a maškim in the employ of the ugula har-tu-$^{d}$sùd. It is probable that the term maškim which follows the latter anthroponym refers to the three officials which precede it even if there is no existing reference to ur-é-nun-gal as a maškim.

lugal-ezen lùmgi should be identified with the person of the same name in the employ of the é-géme in **147** r. IV 4-5 as can be deduced from the following passages: nam-mah lugal-ezen in **116** v. III 12-13; **121** v. V 13-14; nam-mah lugal-ezen é-géme in **147** r. IV 3-6; nam-mah lùmgi in **76** r. III 4-5; **77** v. I 3-4; **89** r. I 6-II 1; **104** r. II 3-4 and **152** r. II 3-4.

We should consider that all these officials, even though they have different professions, must have belonged to a single office, perhaps the é-géme, and were the direct subordinates of the sanga-GAR.

8) The eighth group (r. V 8-v.I 2) lists three officials: kun-du$_6$, KA-ni-zi sagi, munus-u$_4$-ba muhaldim. Kun-du$_6$ is mentioned as sagi in a barley text of the II group **29** r. VII 9-10, in a text concerning anše, **132** v. VII 9-10 and in a text concerning copper WF 147 r. II 10-III 1. KA-ni-zi is mentioned as sagi in a barley text of the II group **19** r. V 5-6, in a text concerning textile fibres BIN 8, 384 r. III 4; and as a subordinate of the gal-sagi in a text concerning fields **74** v. III 6-7. The professional name refers to both functions. To these two, maš-da$_5$ sagi should be added; he is mentioned together with the first two in **189** v. II 1'-3'. munus-u$_4$-ba muhaldim is not mentioned elsewhere but could

12 It should be observed that from his mention in TSŠ 614 the official in question would seem to have had the role of ugula; while from **3** he seems to be clearly a subordinate of an ugula. This could mean that TSŠ 614 was compiled in a period following that of the I group of the barley texts, probably a few months later. A similar situation seems to exist between the barley texts and some of the anše texts; the same person, utu-ur-sag in **10** r. II 7-8 is a sukkal and receives 2 bariga and 4 bàn and he is a subordinate of the/an ugula, while in **116** r. II 20; **121** v. III 7' and **124** v. I 1 he is described as ugula-sukkal.

be identified with $u_4$-ba, an abbreviation of the same anthroponym, in the employ of the é-géme mentioned in TSŠ 385 r. II' 1'-2'.
The first two officials and maš-$da_5$ must certainly have belonged to the same office together with munus-$u_4$-ba. If the identification of the latter with $u_4$-ba is correct, then that office must have been the é-géme.

9) The ninth group (v. I 3-7) also lists three officials: [d]sùd-anzu, é-šùd-$du_{10}$ dub-sar and nam-mah sipa. [d]sùd-anzu should be identified with the homonymous dub-sar mentioned in many texts both in the I and II groups of the barley texts, a subordinate of the sanga-GAR (**10** r. VI 2'-3'). é-šùd-$du_{10}$, whom our text describes together with the former as a dub-sar, appears to be mentioned with that profession in an anše text (**132** v. V 7-8) and in one concerning fibres (TSŠ 423 r. IV 1-2). He is the scribe who compiled TSŠ 775 (v. I 2). nam-mah sipa should be identified with the engar-sipa of the same name mentioned in TSŠ 522 r. III 2, a class B engar mentioned in the barley texts of the II group (cf. *Šuruppak*, p.101). In addition, this official is mentioned in a text concerning goats, WF 129 r. I 4-5, which, like many of the texts under examination, comes from the site XVII c,d (cf. *infra*, p.86-87). The relationship which seems to exist between these officials escapes us.

10) The tenth group (v. I 8-II 3) lists the following: AN-nu-me é-géme, amar-[d]gú-lá gal nimgir, KA-ni-zi $sa_{12}$-$du_5$. AN-nu-me é-géme should be identified with the engar é-géme mentioned in **135** v. VI 2-3 and with the engar of the énsi mentioned in **11** r. V 5-6. This engar was responsible both for the seed barley of many of the allotment fields and for a very large parcel of land (cf. *Šuruppak*, p.221). amar-[d]gú-lá gal-nimgir is not mentioned elsewhere. KA-ni-zi $sa_{12}$-$du_5$ is mentioned in **36** r. VI 7-8 and he could be identified with the engar of the same name, a subordinate of ur-[d]lamma (cf. **27** r. I 14-16). ur-[d]lamma could then be identified with the $sa_{12}$-$du_5$, one of the officials who headed the administration (cf. *Šuruppak*, p.136).

11) The eleventh group lists the following: GAR-da-nu-tuku, amar-šùba simug, é-DÚR su-$ku_6$, DI-utu sanga-GAR. GAR-da-nu-tuku, in the variant šita-da-nu-tuku, could be identified with the official of the same name mentioned in **19** r.

III 14 who seems to have 11 subordinates. amar-šùba simug and é-DÚR su-$ku_6$ are not mentioned elsewhere. DI-utu sanga-GAR is mentioned in **172** r. VIII 10-13; but it impossible to reach a certain conclusion about this official[13] .

12) The twelfth group (**188** r. IV 1-3; 191 r. II 5'-7') lists three officials: amar-šùba, amar-tùr and amar-nam-nir. amar-šùba should be identified with the ugula é-géme mentioned in **46** r. II 6'; he is mentioned as ugula in a barley text (cf. **11** v.III 8-9) and in an anše text (**134** v. V 8-9). amar-tùr is also to be identified with the ugula é-géme mentioned in sequence with the former in **46** r. II 7'. He is mentioned as ugula in the barley text **23** r. VI 7-8 and in the parallel passages of **24** r. V 7-8 and **25** r. V 3-4, in an allotment field text (**89** r. III 4-6), in two texts concerning anše (**143** r. II 11-12; **151** r. II 1-2) and in a list of persons, NTSŠ 258 v. 2-3. amar-nam-nir should certainly be identified with the ugula-énsi-GAR mentioned several times in the barley texts both of the I group (**13** r. VI 14) and of the II group (**23** r. VI 11-13). He is mentioned as ugula in an anše text (**151** v. I 2-3). In this latter text he was in charge of (or the beneficiary of) the field to which the animals were assigned.
It is probable that these three officials were all ugulas of the énsi and consequently of the é-géme, given the frequent alternation between these two characterizing elements (cf. *infra*, p.114, note 73).

13) The thirteenth group (**191** r. III 3'-6'; **194** r. I 1-4) lists the following: šà-ezen, ur-$^{d}$nin-mú, $^{d}$sùd-anzu and nimgir-teme-na.
These six officials are mentioned in the same sequence in a text concerning SI.NUxŠUŠ:

---

13 **187** lists a twelfth group of 20 men available, described as lú-IGI.NÍGIN (for the meaning of this term cf. *Šuruppak*, p.12, note 13) and subordinates of one official. This official, $^{d}$sùd-anzu, described by the term a-a whose meaning is not clear, is mentioned only twice in the Fara texts; in **14** r. IX and in **29** v. V 3-4. In both cases he is the beneficiary of an allocation of 1 gur of barley.

**TSŠ 969**

r I 1) 385 SI.NUxŠUŠ
2) šà-ezen
3) 370 ur-$^{d}$nin-mú

II 1) 395 $^{d}$sùd-anzu
2) 610 nimgir-teme-na

III blank

v. I 1) šu-nígin
2) 1750[+10 SI.NUxŠUŠ]

This indicates without any doubt that they belong to a single office and, since from other attestations two of these officials are described as šu-ku$_6$,"employed in fishing" (cf. **46** r. IV 1-2: ur-$^{d}$nin-mú šu-ku$_6$; r. IV 5-7; nimgir-teme-na šu-ku$_6$ enku), it is likely that the others are also šu-ku$_6$[14] even if they are not mentioned with that qualification elsewhere. The office to which they belong is probably that of the enku.

14) The fourteenth group (**188** r. II 1-4; **190** r. II 1-4; **192** r. III 5-8) is composed of four officials: mes-lu-lu, dumu-$^{d}$anzu, ad-da and DI-utu. mes-lu-lu is a na-gada mentioned in **15** r. I 7 and in HSS 3, 1 r. V 4-5. In the abbreviated form, lu-lu, he is mentioned as a subordinate of dumu-$^{d}$anzu na-gada in **19** v. I 17-18. In WF 149 he is probably a na-gada, a subordinate of the šùš. dumu-$^{d}$anzu is a na-gada and is mentioned in **19** v. I 18 as well as in **133** r. III 9'-10' and in **134** r. III 3-4. He is mentioned as gu$_4$-gur-SI in **211** r. I 5-6. ad-da should be identified with the sipa-anše šà-uru we have already discussed in the sixth group. DI-utu is the sipa-anše mentioned in **46** r. II 1' and in **19** v. VIII 4-5. It

14 It should be observed that in TSŠ 249 the three šu-ku$_6$ are associated with an ùsan-dù enku; in the same way, in **46** r. IV 3-4 the two šu-ku$_6$ are followed in the same section by an ùsan-dù. It is probable that the ùsan-dù employed in fishing were those who made the nets.

is, therefore, probable that these officials were employed in one or more centres concerned with to the breeding of animals.

15) The fifteenth group (**191** r. IV 2'-4'; **193** r. III 1-3) consists of three officials: a-gestin, é-nu-si and šeš-á-nu-kúš.
It is not possible on the basis of the documentation which has survived to find any element which would enable us to associate these officials with a particular office.

The analysis of the officials mentioned in the 15 groups we have just examined has highlighted the existence of a series of structures to which personnel belonged. These structures are: the offices of the enku, of the sanga-GAR, of the $sa_{12}$-$du_5$ and of the ugula énsi-GAR, of the é-géme, of the é-gal-nimgir, of the KISAL and of the centres for animal breeding.

An attempt to identify the jurisdiction of these offices and their position in the central administrative structure of Fara will be presented in Chapter III in spite of the fact that the total number of their attestations is rather small.

# CHAPTER II

## The Personnel Texts

## §.1 Texts and Commentaries

In this chapter, the remaining 21 texts which record personnel have been examined (cf. *Šuruppak*, p.3)[15] . A fair number of these texts can be associated with the dumu-dumu and the guruš texts, even though they have no direct correlation with them because of their content and their findspot where it has been possible to establish this.

These 21 texts can be sub-divided into two groups. The first group consists of ten texts **(197-206)**; these are general summary texts with few items in which only the number of guruš is indicated followed by the name of the city or the centre of provenance. The remaining eleven texts **(207-217)** are registers which list more detailed items each having the number of guruš and the name of the official in charge generally followed by a characterizing element.

**197 (WF 92)**

r. I 1) 182 guruš
2) unug$^{ki}$

3) 192 adab$^{ki}$
4) 94 nibru$^{ki}$

II 1) 60 lagaš$^{ki}$
2) 56 šuruppak$^{ki}$
3) 86 umma$^{ki}$
4) lú-ba-durun

III 1) KI.EN.GI

**198 (WF 94)**

r. I 1) 140 guruš
2) unug$^{ki}$ lú-dúr

3) 215 adab$^{ki}$
II 1) 74
2) nibru$^{ki}$
3) 110 lagaš$^{ki}$
4) 66 šuruppak$^{ki}$
v. I 1) 128 umma$^{ki}$
blank

---

[15] We have excluded TSŠ 302 and CT 50, 2 from this analysis. TSŠ 302 is difficult to interpret; the recto has been damaged and its typology cannot be clearly defined. For a preliminary discussion in this regard cf. *Šuruppak*, pp. 13-14. CT 50, 2 is to be considered a text of allotment fields (suggestion of P.Steinkeller).

2) DU.DU

3) šu-sum

blank

v. I 1) šu-nígin 670 guruš

2) lú-ba-durun

blank

II 1) an-šè-gú 650 guruš

2) KI.EN.GI lú-dúr

**199 (WF 101)**

r. I 1) 670 guruš-mè DU

2) ninda-kú

3) 1612 guruš

II 1) unken$^{ki}$

2) ninda-kú

3) ì! šeš$_4$

blank

**200 (WF 93)**

r. I 1) 1532 guruš

2) 39 dumu-dumu šitim

II 1) 41 géme

blank

v. I 1) an-šè-gú

2) 1612 lú-ninda kú

II 1) 47 kiš DU

**201 (Š 768)**

r. I 1) [x guruš unug$^{ki}$]

2) 704 adab$^{ki}$

3) 528 nibru$^{ki}$

**202 (Š 935)**

r. I 1) 1502 guruš

2) 25 ugula

3) unug$^{ki}$

4) 787

II 1) 10[+3?] ugula

2) nibru$^{ki}$

3) 660 guruš

4) 11 ugula

5) adab$^{ki}$

| | | |
|---|---|---|
| | 4) 440 lagaš$^{ki}$ | 6) 480 |
| | | III 1) 8 ugula |
| | | 2) lagaš$^{ki}$ |
| I | II 1) [x] um[m]a$^{ki}$ | 3) 480 guruš |
| | | 4) 8 ugula |
| | | 5) umma$^{ki}$ |
| | | v. I 1) 10 nagar |
| | | 2) 10 simug |
| | | 3) 6 ašgab |
| | | 4) šuruppak$^{ki}$ |
| | | 5) [x] šitim |
| | | 6) [x] ad-KID |

The first four texts all come from the site XVII c,d (cf. Martin, *Fara*, p.88) and have already been discussed in *Šuruppak*, pp.10-16. There, the particular correspondence between the summaries of **197** and **200** with the two items in **199** was stressed. The summary of **197** speaks of 670 guruš who came from six Sumerian cities, Uruk, Adab, Nippur, Lagaš, Šuruppak and Umma in that order; this corresponds to the first item of **199** (r. I 1: 670 guruš-mè DU). The summary of **200** mentions 1,612 people (guruš, šitim workers and géme); this correspond to the second item of **199** (r. I 3: 1,612 guruš unken$^{ki}$). This correspondence enables us to insert these documents perfectly within the context of the conscription operation documented in the preceding chapter in relation to a war which does not appear to be exclusively local as the mention of the six Sumerian cities in **197**, **198**, **201** and **202** and of the cities of Unken[16] and Kiš in **199** and **200** seems to indicate.

**197** and **198** list contingents of guruš coming from the same cities listed in the same sequence. **197** adds the phrase KI.EN.GI DU.DU šu-sum before the summary; this can be rendered "the guruš who go to Kiengi have been assigned". After the

16 UNKEN.KI is mentioned in the Geographical List of Ebla, a duplicate of Geographical List of Abu Salabikh (cf. MEE 3, p. 225, 56 v. II 24).

summary there is the term lú-ba-durun, "(these) men (are) resident"[17]. **198** adds the term lú-dúr after the first item regarding the contingent from Uruk; and after the summary only the phrase guruš lú-ba-dúr KI.EN.GI, "the guruš are resident in Kiengi". In spite of the differences between these formulae, the two tablets must refer to similar movements of military personnel who, in different periods but, in all probability, in direct succession, were quartered in KI.EN.GI[18].

**199**, as was previously stated, lists two contingents consisting of 670 and 1,612 guruš. The second contingent (1,612 guruš unken$^{ki}$)[19] besides ninda was supplied with ì šeš$_4$. The line regarding this (v. II 3) was copied by A.Deimel as IR.EREN; this reading was accepted by D.O.Edzard, ZA 66, p.188, sub WF 101, who considered it a PN and by us (cf. *Šuruppak*, p.12). The reading ì šeš$_4$ was suggested by a comparison with an Early Sargonic text from Umma, Nik II, 9, which read: 580 guruš éren-mah 10 ir$_{11}$ énsi-ka 50 géme-ḪAR 15 géme sagi-mah 10 géme é-[ ] 22 [ ] sá-bùm-m[a] ì šeš$_4$ kin-aka 3 iti 9 u$_4$. In both texts, the meaning of this term must be "(supplied with) oil for awointing". For other mentions of ì šeš$_4$ in ED IIIb and Sargonic texts cf. Foster, USP, p.26:

---

17 The reading lú-dab$_5$-dab$_5$-ba, "These are the men engaged" proposed by *Frühe Schrift*, p.121, would not modify substantially the proposed reconstruction.

18 For the meaning of KI.EN.GI in these two texts cf. *Šuruppak*, p.11. For the etymology of this toponym in the subsequent documentation cf. P.Steinkeller, *Early Political Development in Mesopotamia*, in *Akkad*, p.112, note 9.

19 An interesting interpretation of the term UNKEN.KI is suggested to me by P.Steinkeller ".. if so, UNKIN.KI is a technical term, describing a type of work. Since UNKIN is a graph of /kin/ "work" in the Ebla sources, the term is perhaps to be analiyzed as KIN$_x$.KI, "earth-work". Accordingly in **199** (WF 101) the workers are divided into those "who went to battle" (guruš mè DU), and those who were assigned to "earth-works" (KIN$_x$.KI). Note that, according to **200**, the 1612 guruš KIN$_x$.KI included 39 dumu-dumu šitim, which support the idea that KIN$_x$.KI involved some kind of a building activity" (private communication). Such an hypothesis could be supported by the comparison between the amount of guruš, 6580, recorded in the summary of **196** and the total number of men enlisted in **199**, 2282 (men in this hypothesis of Šuruppak), and **202**, 3974 men of other Sumerian cities and 26[+x] craftmen of Šuruppak.

**200** lists two contingents; as we have stated above, the first is made up of guruš, šitim workers and géme whose sum total of 1,612 is mentioned in the colophon with the phrase lú-ninda-kú, "men who eat bread"; the second contingent is mentioned after the summary and is made up of 47 lú-kiš-DU, probably a contingent directed towards Kiš. It cannot be excluded that this contingent was part of the 1,612 listed in the first place and it could be connected with the mention of a gal-šitim of Kiš in TSŠ 782 r. III 8-10; for a discussion of this text cf. Th.Jacobsen, *Early Political Devolpment in Mesopotamia*, ZA 52 (1957), p.121. The 39 dumu-dumu-šitim in r. I 1-2 should certainly be linked to the 40 dumu-dumu-šitim mentioned in TSŠ 81 r.I 1-2 who were beneficiaries of rations of flour[20].

**201-202**, hitherto inedited, have recently been published by H.Steible-F.Yildiz[21]. These two documents are, in our opinion, of considerable importance. In

---

20 It should be observed that the guruš conscripted for military service often receive rations of flour and not of barley probably for logistical reasons. This is mentioned specifically in TSŠ 81 but also in the colophons of **182** and **192**. However, **189**, indicates in the colophon that the men have received rations of barley (še-ba lú šu-ba-ti).

21 H.Steible-F.Yildiz, *Kiengi aus der Sicht von Šuruppak*, Istanbuler Mitteilungen, Band 43 (1993), p.17-27. In this article, besides **201** and **202**, two other unpublished texts are given. Š 243 is considered by the authors to be a text concerning rations; but, in fact, it should be regarded as a register concerning the allocation of anše as can be deduced both from the total of the goods allocated which are given in decreasing order from 4 to 1 (for this characteristic of the anše texts cf. *Šuruppak*, p.303) and especially from the mention of the beneficiaries who recur in almost all texts of this type and also in those of the allotment fields and carts for use in agriculture (for the close relationship between these types of texts cf. *Šuruppak*, p.218; 226; 306-308). The reading kiš$^{ki}$ as the beneficiary of an allocation of two anše in v. I 3 does not convince neither for paleographical reasons (the sign read KIŠ, LAK 248, is in reality LAK 249) nor for reasons connected with the typology the texts belong to. In fact, all the beneficiaries of allocations of anše in the administrative documentation of Fara are identified by means of their anthroponym. In many cases this is followed by a characterizing element. Or they are identified only by the professional name of a high-ranking official. In no case is a beneficiary identified exclusively by the name of a city. Furthermore, the comparison with the lú-kiš$^{ki}$ mentioned in TSŠ 135 does not seem to be pertinent. This latter text is a messenger document discussed by us in *Šuruppak*, p.206;

fact, they record quantitatively the real military commitment not only of Šuruppak but also of the other cities of the Hexapolis. From texts **197** and **198** these numbers appear to have been very limited when compared to the number of guruš conscripted in **187, 188** and **181**. It is possible that the 6580 guruš recordd in **196** represent the total number of men recruited in the six sumerian cities. The two texts appear to be different stages in the recording of the same operation of counting personnel; **201** should be regarded as a first memorandum for such a counting[22] while **202** is more updated and detailed where, for example, the number of guruš is followed by the number of their respective ugulas in the proportion of about 60 to 1. This proportion agrees well with the number of dumu-dumu who make up an im-ru under the leadership of an ugula (cf. *supra*, p.25). The mention of a series of artisans, like for

---

we believe that the sign should be read alim, an abbreviated form of the anthroponym pa$_4$-alim; this individual recurs as a beneficiary both in the texts concerning anše (**134** r. III 12, **138** r. III 2, **143** v. I 2, **170** v. I 4), in those concerning allotment fields (**68** r. VII 8, **72** r. I 6, **73** r. II 2, **86** r. V 3) and in texts which regard carts for use in agriculture (**172** r. IV 15, **173** r. III 11, **174** r. V 3).

Š 954, of which only the upper part of the recto is preserved, is difficult to understand. In the surviving part, it has a list of three officials, two subordinates of the gal-dam-gàr and one of the maškim who should perhaps be identified as the maškim-maškim-gi$_4$ UR.UR (cf. *Šuruppak*, p.421) engaged in activities which are not clearly described. The greatest interest these two documents have is the mention of officials not elsewhere named who come from other cities (ur-kèš$^{ki}$ from Keš) and especially the discovery that many officials and artisans whose names we already knew from the documentation came from cities of the Hexapolis. ur-$^{d}$nin-ri$_8$-ru-a, a sipa $^{d}$sùd, elsewhere a na-gada, is mentioned as a middle-ranking official in texts concerning anše, allotment fields and barley: he comes from Adab; en-šà-ge is a šùš mentioned in a text concerning carts (**172** r. X 8-9): he comes from Kullab.

22 H.Steible-F.Yildiz, art. cit., p.23 believe that the side of the tablet which has survived is the verso and complete the first line thus: gú-[an-šè]. But it is much more probable that this is the recto of the tablet and that the first line recorded, as in **197**, **198** and **202**, the number of guruš from Uruk, a contingent which would otherwise be surprisingly absent. The reduced dimensions of the tablet would make it impossible to record more detailed lists of guruš on the lost side whose summary would then be given on the verso.

example, nagar, simug, ašgab, šitim and ad-KID, all probably from Šuruppak[23], reminds one of "sappers" associated for logistical and military reasons with an expeditionary force coming from the cities of the Hexapolis to the aid of Šuruppak. It is probable that the aim of the records in **201** and **202** is the same as that in **196**, namely, the need to estimate the sustenance needed for such a large number of people temporarily not engaged in productive activity[24].

| **203 (TSŠ 554)** | | | | **204 (TSŠ 780)** | | |
|---|---|---|---|---|---|---|
| r. | I | 1) | 53 guruš | r. | I | 1) 60[+30] l[ú]-zà[h] |
| | | 2) | šà-é-gal | | | 2) šà-é-gal |
| | | 3) | 55 guruš | | | 3) 104[+x?] lú-zàh šà-uru |
| | II | 1) | šà-uru | | II | 1) [60?+]27 UN.TAR KI.RA.AŠ |
| | | | blank | | | 2) šà é-gal |
| | | | | | | 3) 70 UN.TAR šà-uru |
| v. | I | | blank | | | blank |
| | II | 1) | šu-nígin | v. | I | blank |
| | | 2) | 108 | | | |
| | | 3) | lú-zàh | | II | 1) an-šè-gú 177 šà-é-gal |
| | | | | | | 2) [x+]117 šà-uru |
| | | | | | | blank |

---

23 The transcription of the šitim and the ad-KID after the mention of Šuruppak can only mean that they were added to the list after the tablet had been compiled.

24 In this context TSŠ 50 and 671, hitherto considered to be only scholastic texts (cf. M.Powell, in J.Friberg, *Mathematics*, p.115) could have quite a different meaning. In fact, what has been recorded in the two texts appears to be a realistic and not a theoretical evaluation of the amount of food needed for the sustenance not only of the military contingent engaged in war but also of the population of the city.

| **205 (TSŠ 613)** | | | **206 (TSŠ 501)** | | |
|---|---|---|---|---|---|
| r. | I | 1) 186 guruš | v. | I | 1) 86 lú šà-uru! |
| | | 2) šà-é-uru DU | | | 2) 41[+x] [šà-é-gal] |
| | | | | | 3) [ ] |

These four documents relate to military contingents recruited from among the personnel of the administrative centres é-gal and é-uru.

**203** lists two contingents; one šà-é-gal and the other šà-uru. These are indicated collectively in the colophon as lú-zàh, "men who have fled or have been dispersed", in all probability related to the warfare in progress.

**204** lists two contingents, one šà-é-gal and the other sà-uru; both of these are indicated as lú-zàh. Two other contingents are also listed who come from the same administrative centres and are indicated as UN.TAR; this is probably a military term whose meaning escapes us. The term KI.RA?.AŠ in r. II 1 which describes the first UN.TAR contingent could indicate a toponym. The colophon has two summary items relative to the two centres, é-gal and é-uru; each of these should contain the total of the lú-zàh and UN.TAR contingents but the sum of each of these does not seem to agree with the sum of the surviving numbers of each of the items.

**205** records a contingent described as šà-é-uru DU; the meaning is probably similar to that of the formula šà-é-uru of **203-204** and guruš-mè DU of **199**.

**206** is a small fragment and has only one line which TSŠ copies as šà-lú-tuku. Since there is no mention in the documentation of Fara of a profession tuku, we have preferred the reading uru instead of tuku in consideration of the number of men recruited and in comparison with the items of the preceding texts.

**207 (TSŠ 933)**

v. I 1) an-šè-gú 83 guruš é-AŠ.SAG.DÙ

The meaning of the term é-AŠ-SAG-DÙ escapes us and is never mentioned elsewhere. Perhaps it could be regarded as made up of the anthroponym é-AŠ.SAG and the verbal form DÙ. é-AŠ.SAG is a subordinate of the dub-sar dumu-nun-šita mentioned in TSŠ 649 r. I 2-3; he was perhaps a dub-sar himself according to the colophons of **182**, **212** and **213**. The dub-sar Dumununšita is mentioned again in WF 135 v. I 4-5, of whom da-dum lú-$^{giš}$u$_5$ is a subordinate, and II 3-4.

**208 (WF 96)**

r. I 1) 18 guruš
2) lú-lum-ma
3) 18 é-na-lu-lu
4) KA-nun-zi
5) ugula
6) šeš-bala-gal

This document comes from the site XVII c,d and lists two contingents of 18 guruš each; in charge of them are lú-lum-ma and é-na-lu-lu who were probably two officials, the subordinates of KA-nun-zi, the ugula of the šeš-bala-gal, a professional name which is also applied to Ena-lulu in a list of persons but whose precise meaning escapes us (cf. WF 42 r. III 2-5: KA-ni-zi dumu é-na-lu-lu šeš-bala-gal)[25] . KA-nun-zi is also mentioned but without a characterizing element in **195** r. VIII 3 as the official of whom pa$_4$-á-nu-kúš is a subordinate and in **52** r. I 5 as the beneficiary of

[25] A professional name šeš-gal is mentioned in a text from the time of Lugalzagesi: BIN 8, 57 r. II 5 and in two other documents from Early-Sargonic Umma: Nik II, 14.3; USP, 1.3. R.B.Foster has proposed for this term a general translation "foreman" (cf. USP, p.18). This interpretation agrees well with some mentions in the Ur III documentation (cf. M.Sigrist, SUL 386 v. 1: ur-$^d$su'en du-a-mu ku-li šeš-gal nam-10-me; MVN 15, 389.2: ur-ku šeš-gal lú-hun-gál-me). But in another mention the term šeš-gal seems to be connected with the religious sphere (cf. F.Yildiz-T.Gomi, *Die Umma teste aus den archäologischen Museen zu Istanbul, Band III (nr.1601-2300)*, Bathesda 1993, 1750 seal: dur-e$_{11}$-e dumu ù-ma-ni šeš-gal $^d$ùr-bar-tab).

allocations of seed barley. It is probable that this document both because of its structure and its findspot should be considered a recruitment text of the šeš-gal-bala.

**209 (TSŠ 292)**

r. I 1) [1] [ ]
2) unug[ki]
3) 1 [ ]
4) unug[ki]
5) 1 nimgir-mete-na
6) unug[ki]

II 1) [1] ] ]
2) [unug[ki]]
3) [1] [ ]
4) unu[g][ki]
5) 1 utu-šita
6) šu-i
7) unug[ki]

III 1) [1 ur-dumu-zi]
2) [unug[ki]]
3) blank
4) lú-má
5) uru-$kas_4$

v. I-II blank

III 1) an-šè-gú 8 lú-má
2) šà-$addir_x$-aka

This tablet has reached us seriously damaged as a result of a breakage in the upper right-hand part of the recto. The summary mentions eight lú-má šà-$addir_x$-

aka,"eight boatmen in charge of the rudder ?". The anthroponyms of two of these with their characterizing element have survived; of the other three, only this latter element has survived. In all five cases the characterizing element is the name of the city of Uruk; in the case of utu-šita, r. II 5-7, this element is preceded by the professional name, šu-i. At the end of the list (r. III 4-5) all the subordinates are indicated as lú-má uru-$kas_4$. A similar indication describes a list of 7 anthroponyms in the last section of **23** (v. IV 15-V 5) where the characterizing element of the various individuals mentioned is the name of a city (Adab, Kullab, Umma and Uruk). The two surviving anthroponyms of our text recur together with ur-dumu-zi in this list followed by the name of the city of Uruk. There is no mention in the surviving documentation of the five other lú-má officials from Uruk which our text ought to have listed; thus, it is impossible to propose any other integration apart from ur-dumu-zi.

This text, which could be linked to the items of **197** r. I 1-2 and **198** r. I 1-2, is also probably connected with the operation of recruitment.

## 210 (TSŠ 765)

r. I 1) 1 KA-zi
2) 1 AN-nu-me
3) 1 ní-$zu_5$-kur-šè
4) 1 lú-$su_{13}$
5) 1 dumu-$^d$anzu
6) $gu_4$-gur-SI
7) 1 zà-ta

II 1) [1 $^d$sùd-anzu$^?$]
2) 1 [ur-]sipa
3) 1 [en]-nu-[kur-šè]
4) 1 ba-zi
5) 1 unken-a
6) é-lugal
7) 1 pa-$bil_x$-ga

III 1) [1 ]
2) 1 na-ni
3) é-$gu_4$
blank

IV 1) dub-udu-še-kú
blank

v. I-II blank

III 1) na-gada
2) 5 $gu_4$-gur-SI
3) 6 é-lugal
4) 3 é-$gu_4$
blank

IV 1) šu-nígin
2) 14 na-gada
blank

The text lists 15 na-gada who are sub-divided into three groups and described, respectively, by a professional name $gu_4$-gur-SI and by the names of two centres é-lugal and é-$gu_4$.

The name of one of the 15 na-gada listed in the text is lost, while two others are partially abrased. In the commentary on **37**, a barley text of the II group, we drew attention to r. IV 11-19; this is a sequence of 7 anthroponyms most of whom are mentioned in other texts as na-gada, subordinates of *ba-la*/$bala_x$, a dam-gàr mentioned in **143** r. III 5-6. They are KA-zi, $^d$sùd-anzu, unken-a, en-nu-kur-šè, ur-sipa, zà-ta and NI.NI. The three surviving anthroponyms of our text, zà-ta, KA-zi and unken-a coincide with anthroponyms in this list and the surviving signs enable us to integrate the anthroponyms partially abrased in the text [ur]-sipa[26] and [en]-nu-

[26] TSŠ r. II 1'-2' copies [ ] 1 / sipa which would suggest that sipa is the profession of the PN lost in the lacuna. The comparison with a list in **37** indicates that sipa is a part of the

[kur-šè]. This implies that the list of officials who were subordinates of the *ba-la* in **37** coincides with the list of the na-gada who belong to the é-lugal in our text[27].

**211 (TSŠ 931)**

v. I' 1') KA-ni-[ ]
2') nimgir
destroyed

II' 1') mes-[é]-zi-da ugula
2') 1 im-ru-a
3') ta-ta
destroyed

III' 1') [ ]
2') utu-[ur]-sag
3') mu-ni-da
4') AN-nu-me
5') munus-á-nu-kúš
6') šeš-tur ugula
7') blank

IV' 1) blank
2) nam-mah
3) šeš-tur

---

PN ur-sipa and that there was no line of separation between line 1' and 2'. Conseguently 1 that precede sipa is the *personelkeil* of ur-sipa.

27 Five of the na-gada é-lugal are also mentioned in CT 50, 25, a text concerning goats or guruš whose findspot is probably XVII c,d. Mentioned are unken-a (r. II' 2'), ur-sipa (r. III' 2'-3'), en-nu-kur-šè (r. III' 4'), zà-ta (r. IV 5') and ba-zi (r. V 1-2). The same text also mentions some subordinates of these na-gada who also probably belonged to the same centre.

4) blank

V' 1') blank
2') lu[gal]-á-mah
3') dub-sar

Only the verso of this tablet has reached us; the upper right-hand part is badly damaged. From the surviving lines, the document seems to be a census of the staff of some administrative units, im-ru-a, for which the ugulas mes-é-zi-da and šeš-tur are responsible. These are mentioned in other texts with the same qualifications. The meaning of the mention of nam-mah šeš-tur in v. IV' 1-2 escapes us; it is not followed, as in v. II' 1' and III' 1-2, by an indication of the official in charge. It is probable that it is an addition to the preceding group of which the ugula in charge is šeš-tur. lugal-á-mah is the compiler of the tablet and perhaps also in charge of **the** sustenance of the personnel listed. In fact, he is one of the dub-sars mentioned in **38** and **39**, two barley texts of the III group, whose provenance is from the site XVII c,d. These dub-sars were responsible for large quantities of barley (cf. *Šuruppak*, p.177-178).

## 212 (TSŠ 49)

r. I 1) 1 KA.Ú
2) gala
3) 1 nam-tur
4) gala
5) 1 lam-ma
6) 1 é-zi-pa-è

II 1) dub-sar
2) 1 ur-dumu-zi
3) si-dù
4) 1** é-na-lu-lu
5) na-gada

6) 1** šir-ezen
7) 1 ⌈túl⌉-sag-dúr-du$_{10}$
8) kin-nir

III 1) 1 šubur
2) sa$_{12}$-du$_5$
3) 1 nam-mah
4) GAR-da-lu
5) 1 lugal-hé-gal
6) engar
7) 1 úr-NI
8) munu$_4$-mú

IV 1) 1 kala[m]-du$_{10}$
2) 1** a-zu-zu
3) AN-nu-me
4) abzu-ki-du$_{10}$
5) 1 šubur
6) a-geštin
7) 1** lam-ma
8) á-[u]tu$^?$

v. I 1) 1 ur-kin-nir
2) 1** ur-dumu-zi
3) šeš ur-kin-nir
4) blank

II blank

III 1) blank
2) dub
3) ur-kin-nir
4) en-ki-zi-da
blank

IV 1) blank
2) an-šè-gú
3) 18 lú-gibil
4) apin-d[ù$^{?}$]

This text has survived practically intact. According to the summary in v. IV 2, there are eighteen officials. These have been identified by their anthroponyms and by their characterizing element which in some cases is a professional name (dub-sar, engar, gala, munu$_4$-mù, na-gada and sa$_{12}$-du$_5$) and in others the anthroponym of an official of a higher rank. Some of these (in the order in which they are mentioned KA-ù gala, é-zi-pa-é dub-sar, ur-dumu-zi si-dù, šubur sa$_{12}$-du$_5$, ùr-NI munu$_4$-mù and GAR-da-lu) recur as beneficiaries in the texts concerning lands and anše and also in the barley texts. After the summary, the colophon adds lú-gibil apin-dù, "18 new men who work with the plough". Clearly the eighteen lú-gibil are not the officials mentioned in the text but their subordinates. The meaning of the phrase lú-gibil apin-dù is not very clear; it could mean that the 18 workers were assigned to substitute others to work in the fields with the plough or, more probably in our opinion, they were freshly recruited from among those who worked with the plough in the fields. In this latter case, our text could be compared to **192** and **195**, the two texts which list the guruš conscripted from among those who worked the aša$_5$-šuku. It should be noted that both **192** and **195** have no items in common with each other or with the following **212**. The ur-kin-nir en-ki-zi-da to whom the tablet is attributed was probably responsible for the sustenance of the conscripted men; he should be identified with the dub-sar-aša$_5$ mentioned in a contract (cf. SRJ, p.31, v. I 2-3).

## 213 (CT 50, 3)

r. I 1) 2 guruš
2) amar-$^{d}$izkur
3) 1 é-kur-ra-unken-a
4) 1 é-ki-du$_{10}$-ga
5) 1 ad-da

II 1) 1 AK-dsùd
2) ad-NE
3) 1 amar-tur
4) 1 šubur
5) 1 ur-nin-mú

v. I 1) 1 nam-[m]ah
2) [A]K-[sipa]
3) 1 šà-gú-ba
4) [ ]

II 1) 1 ⌜har⌝-tu-dsùd
2) ur-tur
blank

This tablet, with two columns on the recto and two on the verso, lists 11 items. Six of the eleven anthroponyms mentioned have correspondences with two texts concerning wool, RTC 9 and 11[28]. This is certainly to be linked to the finding of other texts concerning wool in the site XVII c,d (cf. *infra*, §.2). Consequently, **213** seems to be related to the operation of recruitment and probably comes from the site XVII c,d like the other text from the British Museum, **188**.

**214 (TSŠ 525)**

r. I 1') [ ] gišgal?
2') [x+]6 ⌜X⌝-[ ]
3') [ ] di-[utu]
4') ugula-dumu

5') [ ] lú-GIŠ$^?$.DU$_{10}$$^?$
6') [l]ú-má

II 1) [ ] pa$_4$$^?$-é-GIŠ.ÙH
2) lú-má-gur$_8$
3) 30 hur-sag-šè-mah
4) 30 ušum-ki-du$_{10}$
5) kínda

II 1) 30 AN-nu-me
2) maš-$^d$sùd
3) 30 ur-é-nun-gal
4) ama-bára-si
5) 20[+x] ur-$^d$sùd

Only one side of this text, probably the recto, has survived and it has lacunae in the first column. We have regarded the tablet as a personnel document but it cannot be completely excluded that this is a text concerning sheep or SI.NUxŠUŠ when one considers the amount of the goods allocated in the single items. People connected with boats are always mentioned in the SI.NUxŠUŠ texts (cf. *Šuruppak*, p.206); thus the mention of two lú-má in our text could lead us to attribute it to the SI.NUxŠUŠ typology. However, the anthroponyms mentioned do not seem to occur in the texts concerning sheep and SI.NUxŠUŠ. Some of the officials mentioned, DI-utu ugula, ušum-ki-du$_{10}$ kìnda, AN-nu-me maš-$^d$sùd and ur-é-nun-gal ama-bára-si recur in texts concerning anše; hur-sag-šè-mah who precedes ušum-ki-du$_{10}$ kínda should be identified with the homonymous kínda mentioned in a text concerning copper artifacts (WF 147 r. II 1-2) coming from the site XVII c,d. The two officials lú-GIŠ$^?$.DU$_{10}$$^?$ lú-má and pa$_4$$^?$-é-GIŠ.ÙH lú-má-gur$_8$ are not mentioned elsewhere.

## 215 (WF 103)

r. I 1) 1 ki-ni-du$_{10}$
2) maškim adab$^{ki}$
3) 1 ku-li-kalam
4) maškim kèš$^{ki}$
5) 1 MI-mud
6) maškim IM$^{ki}$
blank

The three anthroponyms mentioned in this text do not recur elsewhere with the qualification of maškim. The mention of these officials as coming from Adab, Kèš and IM should link this document, found in the site XVII c,d, with **197** and **198** (for the location of the toponym IM$^{ki}$ cf. RGTG I, p.78).

## 216 (TSŠ 467)

r. I 1) 1 mes-ki-na
2) 1 a-si$_4$
3) 1 maš-lugal
4) 1 maš
5) 1 lugal-ki-gal-la

II 1) 1 a-ki-gal
2) 1 šeš-geštin
3) 1 šita
4) 1 MU-⌈X⌉
5) 1 [ur?]-é-nu[n]-[gal] / é-[a]-nu[n]
6) 1 AN-n[u-me]
7) 1 [ur]-dumu-z[i]

III 1) 1 AN-nu-me
destroyed

v. I 1') [ ] [KA]-lu[gal-da-zi]
2') gal-nimgir
3') [ ] $bil_x$-á-[nu]-kúš
4') šeš-nin
5') blank

II 1) 6[+x] [ ]-érím
2) 7 ama[r]-[ ]
3) 6 luga[l]-da-na?
4) 1 sipa
5) blank

III blank

The tablet has reached us without the lower part of the recto and the upper right-hand part of the verso. All the items, with the exception of the three in v. II 1-3, feature the presence of an oblique wedge which should indicate, in this specific text, the numeral 1[29]. The anthroponyms mentioned, with the exception of the two mentioned in v. I 1'-3', are not followed by a characterizing element; for this reason, it is impossible to identify them. Of the above-mentioned two, $bil_x$-á-nu-kúš šeš-nin is not mentioned elsewhere; KA-lugal-da-zi gal-nimgir is mentioned both in a barley text and in texts concerning fields and anše.

## 217 (WF 99*)

r. I 1) 4 [ ]
2) [ ]
3) [ ]
4) 1 [ ]

---

29 For a different use of the oblique wedge in the administrative documentation of Fara cf. *Šuruppak*, p.68.

5) 5[+x] ⌈har?⌉-⌈tu?⌉-[dsù]d?
6) 1[+x+] šubur
7) lú-⌈zàh⌉

II 1) [ ]
2) [ ]
3) [ ]
4) [ ]
5) 1 [dsù]d-[ur-sag?]
6) 2 lugal-ezen
7) 1 ⌈x-x⌉

III destroyed

v. I-II blank

III 1) an-šè-gú
2) 19 guruš
3) lú-zàh

This text consists of three columns on the recto and three on the verso; there are large lacunae in the upper part of the recto and some of the signs are barely legible. The mention of šubur and lugal-ezen as the officials in the charge of the dispersed men makes it possible for us to suppose that this text should be added to the group of dumu-dumu texts (**181-186**) with the consequent uncertain integrations of r. I 5 and II 5. The phrase guruš lú-zàh, on the other hand, would link this text to **203-204**.

## §.2 The function of the site XVII c,d

The site XVII c,d is situated at the northern extremity of the inhabited area. As can be seen from the excavation report, 96 tablets were found there. The painstaking work of H.P.Martin has recently enabled us to identify 22 of the 96 texts found there (cf. Martin, *Fara*, p.88 Table 16) all of which are to be found in the Berlin Museum. According to the typology to which they belong, they are as follows:

a) Personnel texts: **182**, **184**, **187**, **192**, **193**, **195**, **197-200**, **215** (11 texts);
b) Texts concerning different goods: WF 118, 150, 152 (3 texts);
c) Texts concerning sheep: WF 129, 134 (2 texts);
d) Text concerning wool: WF 132 (1 text);
e) Texts concerning barley: **38-40** (3 texts);
f) Text concerning copper: WF 147 (1 text);
g) Text concerning $ninni_5$: WF 144 (1 text).

To the texts of type a) Martin, *Fara*, p.93 adds **208** probably on the basis of its content, although this is not precisely described.

In the previous chapters we have stressed the extremely close relationship which exists between the dumu-dumu texts and the guruš texts. It has been stated that if one group of documents presents such precise correlations, then all the texts of the group must come from the same findspot. This has been demonstrated in the case of the barley texts of the I and II groups, for those of the allotment fields, for the anše and carts all of which come from the Tablet House. Similary the barley texts of the III group come from the site XVII c,d. It seems evident that this criterion should also be valid for texts of other typologies for which the above-mentioned type of correlation has been ascertained, namely, those texts concerning oil, wool, sheep and fibres (cf. *Šuruppak*, p.22-24) and finally for the recruitment of personnel texts discussed above. We can, therefore, conclude that not only must **181**, **183**, **185**, **186**, **188-191**, **194** and **201-206** and **217** come from the site XVII c,d but also the remaining texts 196, **207**, **209-214** and **216** (a similar hypothesis was advanced by Martin, *Fara*, p.89 in the case of the texts **203-205**).

The texts of type e) **38-40** list considerable quantities of barley. This barley, as was shown (cf. *Šuruppak*, pp.177-178), was the responsibility of some dub-sars. Keeping in mind that **182** lists dumu-dumu personnel under the responsibility of the dub-sar a-hu-ti as indicated in the colophon, and that **195**, **207**, **210-212** contain a similar clause in the colophon we can reasonably conclude that the barley in the charge of the dub-sars in **38-40** was destined for the contingents who had been recruited[30] . Consequently, we must accept that the other texts which H.P.Martin has indicated as coming from the site XVII c,d must have recorded goods which had the same destination. Thus, on the one hand, WF 118 and 152, both belonging to the category of the allocation of different types of goods (the former artifacts in copper, a cart, a quantity of še-gin, "glue", hides of various types, fibres, textiles, various types of beverages, a net for fish and a fish-trap etc, the latter oxen, various types of sheep, different quantities of oil, flour, grain, gahar šu-tag, "cheeses", fruit, wine, dates and beverages in different kinds of containers) without any indication of the beneficiary are an example of registers of this kind; on the other hand, WF 147, a text concerning copper artifacts, lists seven beneficiaries, at least two of whom, kun-du$_6$ sagi and hur-sag-šè-mah, recur in the recruitment texts, the former in **187** r. II 8 and **189** v. II 1' and the latter in **214** r. II 3.

Having established that the documents found in the site XVII c,d are records of goods to be related to the operation of conscription, we can draw other conclusions from the categories of the other texts indicated by H.P.Martin.

---

30 It seems fairly clear that **41** which, like **38** and **40**, mentions considerable quantities of barley, must come from the site XVII c,d. **41**, as was remarked in the commentary on **195**. It lists two quantities of barley, the first of 1560 gur and the second of 46 gur. We have already discussed the destination of the latter (cf. *supra*, p.44). The destination of the former quantity was probably the same as that indicated in **38-40**. In fact, if one considers that the amount of the monthly rations of barley for specialized personnel was 2 bariga and 4 bàn and that for the non-specialized personnel, like the lú-ri-ri-ga, must have been 1 bariga and 2 bàn (cf. *Šuruppak*, p.36), we can calculate, even if only approximately, that the quantity of barley needed every month to feed 6,000/7,000 men, counting the guruš and the personnel of Šuruppak and those recruited from the other Sumerian cities, probably collected in **196**, must have been roughly the same as the total amount mentioned in **41**.

WF 129 is a register with nine surviving items, each of which lists the allocation of a sheep to nine beneficiaries. It has many correspondences with CT 50, 21-22 and TSŠ 385. These latter texts are, in their turn, in reciprocal correlation with a whole series of documents of the same type: CT 50, 19-20; TSŠ 212; 499; 536; 548 and 927. Considering what has already been said, it is likely that all these documents, correlated with one another, come from the same site XVII c,d.

WF 132 is a wool text and has some items in common with RTC 10; like the previous case, this document, in its turn, is related to RTC 9; 11; CT 50, 16; 17 and 25. It should be remembered that RTC 9 and 11 are related to **213**, as has been shown in the commentary on this text. Another text of this type, TSŠ 664[31], mentions three of the five officials in charge of breeding who are mentioned in the guruš texts **188**, **190** and **192**.

WF 144 is a small register of $ninni_5$ and is the only document of this type preserved in the Berlin Museum. It is grouped in the *Sammeltafel* TSŠ 627 together with WF 142, TSŠ 415 and probably also with TSŠ 369 and 736 (cf. G.Visicato, *Some Aspects of the Administrative Organization of Fara*, Or 61 [1992], p.94-99). In addition, another text of this type, TSŠ 969, lists, in the same sequence, a group of šu-$ku_6$ mentioned in **192** and **194**. As well as this, all the texts concerning SI.NUxŠUŠ and $ninni_5$, "fish nets and fish-traps"[32], are related to one another (cf. *Šuruppak*, p.23); many of the beneficiaries of SI.NUxŠUŠ are "foreign" lú-má; and in another *Sammeltafel* of this type, TSŠ 430 r. V' 3'-4', lú-má-mè a-hu-ti are mentioned, probably recruited for war.

So, we can conclude, on the basis of what has been said above that it is likely that all the texts concerning SI.NUxŠUŠ and $ninni_5$ and a large number of the texts concerning sheep and wool come from the site XVII c,d. This means that a sizeable part of the 96 texts which were found in the site XVII c,d, according to the

---

31 TSŠ 664 r. I 1-4: 9 udu-síki mes-lu-lu 10 dumu-$^{d}$anzu 10 ad-da. In the verso of the text, next to the quantity mentioned, the residual quantity is given of the previous count concerning one of the officials named in the recto (cf. TSŠ 664 v. I 1-3: 12 ad-da nì-$kas_7$ libir).

32 For this meaning cf. J.Bauer, *Altsumerische Wirtschaftsurkunden in Leningrad*, Afo 36/37 (1989/1990), p.90 *ad* 278 I 1

archeological expedition's report, can be identified and should be added to the 22 already identified by H.P.Martin. Summarizing, these are:

a) Personnel texts: **181-217** (37 texts);
b) Texts concerning various goods: WF 118; 150; 152; TSŠ 782 (4 texts).
c) Texts concerning sheep: WF 129; 134; TSŠ 212; 385, 499; 548; 536; 927; CT 50, 19-22 (12 texts).
d) Texts concerning wool: WF 132; TSŠ 664; CT 50, 16; 17; 25; RTC 9-11 (8 texts)[33].
e) Texts concerning barley: **38-41** (4 texts).
f) Texts concerning copper: WF 147 (1 texts).
g) Texts concerning SI.NUxŠUŠ and $ninni_5$: WF 142; 144; TSŠ 369; 415; 420; 424; 430; 627; 736; 748; 752; 969 (12 texts)[34].

Counting also TSŠ 725 and DP 36 the total of the texts identified out of the 96 found may be 80[35].

---

33 TSŠ 725 which lists quantities of wool coming from Umma and Uruk could also come from the site XVII c,d.

34 One cannot exclude that DP 36, a Fara-type text concerning SI.NUxŠUŠ of unknown provenance but with a structure similar to TSŠ 424, could also be added to this list.

35 Among the 80 documents for which we have proposed the identification of the findspot we have included 9 texts preserved in the British Museum and published in CT 50 (1; 3; 16; 17; 19-22; 25) and 5 preserved in the Louvre (three of which were published in RTC and two in DP). All of these come from the black market. To these should certainly be added BIN 8, 384 which has a large number of correspondences with different guruš texts. It cannot be excluded that all or a fair number of the Fara-type administrative texts with the exception of contracts bought on the black market, that is, the remaining texts of CT 50, with perhaps the exception of 24 (a text which is paleographically close to the Fara documentation but in other regards extraneous) and DP 33, could come from the site XVII c,d. This would be in agreement with the fact that there does not seem to be any discrepancy between the number of texts found according to the expedition's report and that of the texts preserved in the Berlin and Istanbul Museums. This hypothesis, if verified, could make the identification of all of the 96 texts found in the site XVII c,d possible.

We can draw another conclusion from the identification of the many texts found in the site XVII c,d. If all the texts found in this site are related to one another, in the sense already explained, and they are all concerned with the conscription of soldiers which is recorded in the recruitment texts analysed in the first two chapters, then this site cannot be considered, as H.P.Martin holds, the "archives of a palace or other large political body" (Martin, *Fara*, p.97), even if, as she observes in the following page, "The building consisted of many small rooms; communication between these rooms is not clear on the plan. No courts or rooms with special functions can be distinguished."(cf. *ibidem*, p.98). Without any doubt, the administrative centre of ED IIIa Šuruppak cannot but be situated in the central zone of the area between trenches XV and XIII and the Tablet House seems to be the archives of the central administration. The site XVII c,d should be regarded as an administrative centre used for military purposes as the texts so far analysed seem to indicate. In other words, the site XVII c,d was the headquarters of the logistical organization of the army which, as we can gather from the texts, was mobilized for war. The battle front must not have been very far from the city as can be deduced from TSŠ 782 where it is recorded that soldiers and equipment of this army were moved towards and away from the front line. A confirmation that this area was used for military purposes can be found in the typology of the few finds from this site; H.P.Martin thus comments:"The shafthole axe and spear point represent the type, but not the number, of the objects which we would expect to find in a military center" (cf. *ibidem*, p.99).

# CHAPTER III

## Administrative Centres and Central Offices

The classification of the officials who supplied personnel for recruitment mentioned both in the dumu-dumu texts and in those concerning the guruš has enabled us to identify, on the one hand, about 40 im-ru which seem to have been the back-bone of the palace administration and, on the other, a series of structures some of which must have belonged to the administrative centre of the é-gal and others to that of the é-uru. Thus, we are in a position, on the basis of the data obtained, to get a more precise picture of the two administrative centres and of their reciprocal relations.

## § 1. The Administration of the é-gal

The most important structure of this administrative centre, when one considers the number of its workers, is constituted by the complex of the im-rus. In fact, we have ascertained, in Chapter I that more than 2000 people belonged to these structures. But text **1**, which we have regarded as a monthly summary of the administration of the é-gal, lists, on its surviving side, in addition to the dumu-dumu personnel, the following:

a) nimgirs and the uru-DU personnel. These officials belonged to the office of the gal-nimgir;

b) dam-gàrs and their subordinates. These officials belonged to the office of the gal-dam-gàr;

c) galas (with šà-zu, géme-kar-gé, nu-gig and sa-HAR) who belonged to the office of the gala-mah;

d) dub-sars most of whom must have belonged to the office of the é-géme.

### 1) <u>The Office of the gal-nimgir</u>

The organizational system of this office has, at least in some sectors, close analogies with that of the im-ru. They were, in fact, administrative units; for each of these there was an official in charge, in this case a nimgir. But while the im-ru of the é-gal were structures of a corporate type, as we saw in the previous chapter, where the ugula in charge carried out the same professional activity as his subordinates even though at a different level, the personnel of the administrative units were of different types. The nimgirs were at the top; their subordinates, the uru-DU personnel, generally had a characterizing element which was the name of a city (for the provenance of the uru-DU from the various Sumerian cities cf. *Šuruppak*, p.54 Table 1). In some cases, that element was preceded by a professional name, like for example, nar, zadim etc. They should be regarded as "personnel who travelled on behalf of the administration", who guaranteed a communications system and who had the delicate task of being the connective tissue of the Hexapolis. The nu-su personnel were also the subordinates of the nimgir; they were probably female personnel without any clear-cut qualifications. According to the data obtained from **4** and **5**, these administrative units would seem to have been made up of about 20 people from among the uru-DU and the nu-su personnel. It is possible that these units were composed differently but, unlike the case of the im-ru of the é-gal, we have no elements to document this. From the surviving documentation only eight nimgir are mentioned as being in charge of these units and that only in the barley texts of the I group. In the partial summary texts each nimgir is mentioned after a list of uru-DU and of nu-su personnel at the end of each section. But in the primary documentation they recur in single sequences of the following types: a) $PN_1$ GN / nu-su $PN_2$ nimgir; b) $PN_1$ GN / nu-su $PN_2$; c) $PN_1$ $PN_2$ nimgir. In the case of the last-mentioned sequence, one can understand whether the subordinate is an uru-DU or a nu-su only from the amount of barley allocated, 2 bariga 4 bàn for uru-DU or 1 bariga 2 bàn for nu-su (cf. *Šuruppak*, p.33). The eight nimgirs are: a-nun-$^{d}$sùd; AK-$^{d}$utu; é-abzu-làl; $pa_4$-nu-lá/me; ur-dumu-nun; ur-dumu-zi; ur-en-$unu_6$-ŠIM and ur-$^{d}$nu-muš-da. Some of them are mentioned in the primary documentation as beneficiaries themselves of monthly barley rations of 1 gur[36]. In the same documentation šeš-tur nimgir (**10** v. VI 5-6) also appears as a beneficiary; but he is never mentioned as being in charge of uru-DU and nu-su. Like some of the other above-mentioned nimgirs, he is also the beneficiary of parcels of land and of anše. It is probable that only the first eight nimgirs were the officials in charge of the administrative units made up of uru-DU and nu-su personnel. In fact, **1**, the summary text, lists three items relative to the monthly allocations to uru-DU personnel in r. III 3-5. The first of these refers to the

---

36 a-nun-$^{d}$sùd nimgir **13** r. III 4-5; ur-dumu-(nun/zi) nimgir **13** r. I 7-8; ur-$^{d}$nu-muš-da nimgir **13** r. VII 5-6.

personnel listed in **4** who are subordinates of five nimgirs and amounts to 33 gur 2 bariga 4 bàn. The total amount of the following two items, 12 1/2 gur 2 bariga 4 bàn and 7 gur 2 bariga 4 bàn respectively, suggests that no more than three nimgirs should be added to the five in charge of the uru-DU and nu-su of the first item. However, apart from these eight, it is probable that other nimgirs worked within the administration of the gal-nimgir. In fact, other different anthroponyms followed by the qualification nimgir are mentioned in the documentation of Fara even if it is not always certain whether the characterizing element which follows these anthroponyms should be considered as the real profession of the official. In some cases, the nimgir which follows the anthroponym seems to be a variant, or better an abbreviation, of gal-nimgir; this means that the anthroponym thus characterized is a subordinate of the latter and therefore is a part of his administration but not necessarily a nimgir himself. This is the case of the following:

1) é-ki-du$_{10}$-ga nimgir: RTC 9 r. II 2-3; é-ki-du$_{10}$-ga gal-nimgir: TSŠ 423 r. I 5; II 5.
2) KA-lugal-da-zi nimgir: WF 121 r. I 3; KA-lugal-da-zi gal-nimgir: **12** v. I 10-12; **121** r. I 8-9; **123** r. I 1-2; **128** r. III 1-2; **164** r. II 8-III 1.
3) mes-ki-érim nimgir **132** v. VIII 7-8; **135** r. V 8'-9; mes-ki-érim gal-nimgir **116** r. II 7-8.

The most numerous group of officials[37] is that mentioned only with the characterizing element nimgir[38] :

amar-$^{d}$izkur nimgir: RTC 11 v. I 4
amar-amar: TSŠ 524 r. II 1-2[39]

---

[37] Among the officials thus described there are also some of the eight whom we know for certain to have carried out the profession of nimgir in addition to those listed above: a-nun-$^{d}$sùd nimgir (**121** v. II 5'-6'; **122** v. I 4-5; WF 149 r. II 11-12); pa$_{4}$-nu-lá (**116** r. III 19-IV 1; **124** v. V 16-VI 1).

[38] We have not included in this list KA-ni-[ ] nimgir mentioned in **209** v. I' 1'-2' both because it is possible that the sign gal was present in the lacuna beside the sign nimgir and because this element could refer to all the anthroponyms listed in the section which has been lost.

amar-inanna: NTSŠ 262 r. II 1-2
mes-$u_4$-ba: **152** r. I 1-2
$^{d}$sùd-anzu: **86** r. I 4-5; **116** r. III 13-14; **124** v. I 5-6
šeš-tur: **10** v. VI 5-6; **115** r. III 3-4
ur-é -<nun>-gal: **115** v. VI 6-7; **147** r. III 6-8[40]

To these officials two others should be added; they recur in the same sequence PN nimgir and they are only mentioned in contracts where they recur as witnesses:

lú-dingir-mah nimgir: BAOM 5, p.18 r. IV 6-8; MVN 10, 84 r.V 3-5; SEL 3, p.11 v. I 6-8
šeš-kur-ra nimgir: Orient 19, p.2 r. V 1-2

Unfortunately, it is not possible on the basis of the documentation to clarify the activity of these nimgirs. The mention of two nimgir in contracts as witnesses just as the presence of the nimgir-sila in property sale contracts could suggest that the functions of the nimgirs were diversified.

A case of particular interest is that of AK-$^{d}$istaran and $^{d}$sùd-ur-sag. Both officials are described as ugula-nimgir in **122** r. VI 7'-8' and **93** r. I 5-6 respectively; but while the former has gal-nimgir as a characterizing element in NTSŠ 258 v. II 1-2, the latter is mentioned as nimgir-é-al-la in **116** r. IV 4-6. The presence of this variant could lead us to suppose that the é-al/$al_6$-la and the <é>-gal-nimgir were identical. But, in fact, none of the subordinates of the é-al/$al_6$-la mentioned in the documentation of Fara[41] seems to be immediately identifiable with a subordinate of

---

39 The nimgir in r. II 2 seems to refer not only to this anthroponym but also to ur-teme who precedes him in r. I 2. It is probable that here it is a question of the mention of two officials who were subordinates of the gal-nimgir.

40 The comparison between the three sequences har-tu-$^{d}$sùd SAL.UŠ ur-é-gal nimgir (**115** v. VI 6-7), har-tu-$^{d}$sùd ur-é-gal nimgir (**147** r. III 6-8) and har-tu-$^{d}$sùd ur-é-nun-gal (**12** r. II 8-9) shows that the complete anthroponym of this official is the last-mentioned one.

41 The officials of the é-al/$al_6$-la are: AK-$^{d}$nu-mus-da (**124** r. III 17-18; **125** v. VI 6-7); AN-úr-šè (**124** v. IV 13-14; **128** v. IV 2-3; **132** v. III 9-10; **134** v. I 1-2; **135** r. I 6-7; **136** v. IV 9-10); é-pa-è (**36** r. II 4-5); har-tu-$^{d}$sùd nu-$kiri_6$ (**119** r. III 1'-3'); ŠEŠ-ki-na (**117** r. V 3-4;

the nimgir or of the gal-nimgir. It is perhaps possible that $^{d}$sùd-ur-sag was an ugula-nimgir seconded to the office of the é-al/al$_{6}$-la with tasks which escape us just as the exact role of the é-al/al$_{6}$-la escapes us. This centre is sometimes mentioned in the concluding parts of land purchase contracts as the district or the administrative centre of the fields in question. The presence of a nimgir in the office of the é-al-la, just as in that of the KISAL and in the má-lah$_{4}$, could suggest that this é-al-la might also have been connected with the system of comunications.

Other subordinates of the gal-nimgir are mentioned; two with the formula PN Prof.N (gal-)nimgir, namely, nin-ur-sag IB gal-nimgir in NTSŠ 262 r. II 7-III 2 and zà-ta nag-su (gal-) nimgir in **157** r. I 4-5; the remaining ones are mentioned with the more generic PN gal-nimgir[42] .

In addition to the nimgir KISAL of the administration of the nu-bànda (cf. *infra*, p.115-116), four nimgir-sila are mentioned in purchase contracts for houses or building areas. These are: da-da in NSRJ, p.228, 12 v. II 8-9; lugal-KA-ni-nu-šùba in SRJ, 29 v. I 2-3; me-zu/zu$_{5}$-an-da in SRJ, 28 v. II 7'-8'; 25 v. II 5'-6'; ur-é-$^{d}$sàman MVN 10, 85 v. V 6-7. These officials receive retribution for their work (še, ninda, gúg, PAP.HIxAŠ and PAP.NIGINxA.A[43] ); this is inferior only to that due to the lú-é-ès-gàr, the other official who, together with the dub-sar, represents the central administration in this type of private document. The names of these nimgir-sila recur at the end of contracts after that of the lú-é-ès-gàr and before the name of the purchaser and of the official bala who ratified the transaction. One could suppose that the presence of this official in contracts might be linked to a relationship between the building and the street plan, that is, to the rights of the area and access to the

---

**124** v. III 4-5); ŠU-mu (**128** v. III 7-8). To these should be added ad-da-ki-za ad-da-uru, a witness mentioned in a contract (MVN 10, 84 r. III 11-13). Among all those mentioned above only AN-úr-sè could be identified with the homonymous gala mentioned in NTSŠ 118 r. V 1-2 as a subordinate of the gal-nimgir.

42 These officials are: amar-$^{d}$gú-lá (**187** v. I 10-II 1); AN-nu-me (**195** r. IV 1-2); lum-ma (**19** v. VIII 9-10); nam-mah (NTSŠ 118 v. II 4-5); nin-gú-gal (**6** v. IV 4-5).

43 For the meaning of these terms and for the reading tu$_{7}$ of HIxAŠ cf. ELTS, p.293.

building[44]. The interchange in contracts between the nimgir-sila and the gal-nimgir (cf. ELTS, p.204, no.36) indicates without any doubt that the nimgir-sila belonged to the office of the gal-nimgir.

One of the items of **1** records in r. III 6, 26 (gur) nimgir. This item has been interpreted as a monthly allocation for 26 nimgirs (cf. *Šuruppak*, p.33). But, in the light of what has thus far emerged, it should be considered as the barley ration of the VII month for the personnel of the administration of the gal-nimgir. The barley for the uru-DU personnel who also belong to this centre was calculated and recorded separately in the three preceding lines (r. III 3-5). Another allocation of 120[+x] gur of barley and 20[+x] of emmer to the central office of the gal-nimgir is mentioned in TSŠ 247 r. II 4-6. This text is difficult to interpret but it seems to be a list of allocations of barley and emmer to various centres some of which are never mentioned elsewhere, for example, HUL.GÁL (r. I 3), é-a-tu (r. II 1), KA.NI.KIŠ? (v. I 2). Others are mentioned in the documentation of Fara like, en-líl (r. III 3) and A.HA$^{ki}$[45] (v. II 4) but are not easy to locate. The text contains no time notation but the comparison between the quantity of barley allocated monthly to the administration of the nimgir in **1** and that which survives in TSŠ 247 leads us to suppose that this latter text could be a six monthly summary register of different kinds of grain.

Of particular interest is a text concerning the allocations of oil by this office to a series of beneficiaries who all seem to be subordinates of the gal-nimgir.

---

44 For a discussion of the term nimgir-sila cf. NSRJ, pp.176-177. In addition, it should be noted that the mention of the nimgir persists in the purchase contracts of ED IIIb Girsu where the nimgir-sila is mentioned in Fara.

45 The location and function of the centre $^{d}$en-líl will be discussed in the pages which follow in relation to the breeding of cattle cf. *infra*, p.130. We do not know, even if it appears likely, whether the toponym A.HA$^{ki}$ mentioned here is an abbreviation of A.HA.A$^{ki}$ mentioned in TSŠ 864 in relation to megida or whether it should be identified with the city of Ku'ara (cf. RGTC I, pp.95-96 sub Ku'ara). In our opinion, it seems improbable that the toponym mentioned in our texts could be situated in Ku'ara south of Ur. For the location of a city with the name of Ku'ara in the north of the country near Babylon cf. P.Steinkeller, *On the Reading and Location of the Toponyms ÚRxÚ.KI and A.HA.KI*, JCS 32 (1980), p. 27-32.

## NTSŠ 118

r I 1) [ ] sìla ì-nun

2) é-nu-zà

3) 2 $^{d}$sùd-[ ]

4) [ ]

5) 5 šita-nu-nu-gíd

6) 5 har-tu-$^{d}$sùd

II 1) 5 ur-[me]te-[n]a

2) am[ar$^{?}$-amar$^{?}$]

3) 5 [ ]

4) [ ]

5) 5 [ ]

6) 5 nì-kur$_4$-ra

III 1) 5 [m]es-u$_4$-ba

2) [2+]3 [a$^{?}$-n]un$^{?}$-$^{d}$sùd

3) [ ]

4) [ ] [é$^{?}$]-lum$_x$

5) 3[+x] ⸢zà⸣-[t]a$^{?}$

6) [ ] [š]ubur

IV 1) 5 $^{[d]}$sù[d]]-ur-sag

2) 5 [ ]

3) 5 [ ]

4) 5 ŠEŠ-[ ]

5) 5 ⸢amar⸣-inanna

V 1) 2 AN-úr-šè

2) gala

3) [ ]-na

4) [ ]-[H]U$^{?}$

5) [gal]-[ni]mgir

6) blank
7) blank

v. I 1) 20 gal-nimgir
2) 20 galla$^{lá}$
3) 20 má-lah$_4$
4) 10 nu-bànda$^{da}$
5) <gal>-nimgir

II 1) 2 utu-nu-me
2) 5 ur-dumu-nun
3) 5 nin-pirig
4) 3 nam-mah
5) gal-nimgir

III blank

IV 1) blank
2) an-šè-gú
3) [60$^?$+]30 lá 3 ì-[nun]
4) dub ì-è
5) gal-nimgir

V 1) blank
2) 85 sì[la] ì-[nun]
3) gal-nimgir
blank

This tablet has suffered serious damage especially in the recto. It has many lacunae consisting of one long fracture which cuts through the central part and a second in the lower left-hand side. The verso, however, is perfectly legible. The text is divided into two sections (r. I 1-V 5 and v. I 1-II 5) both of which conclude with the notation gal-nimgir[46]. The colophon is also divided into two parts; the first (v. IV 1-4) contains a summary which has largely been lost and the clause dub ì-è [g]al-nimgir, "tablet concerning the delivery of oil (from the office) of the gal-nimgir" and the second (v. V 1-2) notes a quantity of 85 sìla of oil followed by the clause gal-nimgir. Since this quantity coincides with the sum of the eight items listed in the second section[47], it is probable that the summary of the first register must refer to the allocations of oil in the first section even if the reason for two separate summaries corresponding to the two sections of the text escapes us[48]. One could suppose that the second section with its own summary was added when the tablet had already been compiled because the scribe had forgotten to do so earlier. This would explain the fact that the clause dub-ì-è which we would have expected at the end of the second summary is written only at the end of the first. It is also possible that the reason is to be found in accounting procedure as would seem to be the case in **139**.

In any case, the notation at the end of the two sections seems to be precise; the deliveries were reserved for the allocations to the personnel of the gal-nimgir. This is confirmed by the fact that the different anthroponyms mentioned in sections I and II are elsewhere mentioned as subordinates of the gal-nimgir either as nimgir or as uru-DU, their subordinates. More precisely, section I must have listed about twenty beneficiaries; the names of only fifteen of them have survived. Of these, é-nu-za (r. I 2) and šita-nu-nu-gíd (r. I 5) are not mentioned elsewhere, har-tu-$^{d}$sùd (r. I 6)

---

46 In all the administrative documentation of Fara the columns of the verso which continue the list of the goods allocated are written from right to left while the column with the colophon is generally written on the extreme left. If there is more than one column in the colophon, it is written from left to right. This technique of compilation can be seen, for example, in **144**, **147**, **151**, **154** and **201**. A substantially similar scribal practice seems to have been already in use in the Jemdet Nasr period (cf. J.P.Gregoire-R.Englund, *Proto-Cuneiform Texts from Jemdet Nasr*, Berlin (1991), p.9-12) and is also witnessed in the later texts of ED IIIb Girsu (cf. G.Selz, *AWAS*, 67-69; 118-124; 127).

47 D.O.Edzard, ZA 66, p.166 is of the same opinion.

48 With regard to this characteristic, NTSŠ 118 is not unique in the administrative documentation of Fara. Also in **139**, a register of anše (cf. *Šuruppak*, p.391), there are two summaries in the colophon. These correspond to two sections of the document; the first concerns the dam-gàr and the second personnel with various professions.

is mentioned in **115** v. VI 4-7 as the SAL.UŠ of ur-é-nun-gal, ur-mete-na (r. III 1) as a subordinate of amar-amar nimgir in TSŠ 524 r.I 1-3 (cf. *supra*, p.94), mes-$u_4$-ba (r. III 1) is characterized by the element nimgir in **152** r. I 2-3, [a-nu]n-$^{d}$sùd (r. III 2) is a nimgir mentioned in a barley text of the I group, zà-ta (r. III 5) is the nag-su of the (gal)-nimgir in **157** r. I 4-5, [ur-du]mu-[z]i (r. IV 2) could be identified either with the homonymous nimgir mentioned in **9** v. II 3-4; **12** r. VII 16; v. II 15-16; **13** r. III 2-3 or with the uru-DU mentioned in **4** r. II 2-3, amar-inanna (r. IV 6) with the nimgir mentioned in NTSŠ 262 r.II 1-2 and AN-úr-sè gala with the nar unug$^{ki}$ of **4** r. IV 10-12. In addition, šubur (r. III 5) could be the uru-DU mentioned in **4** r. VII 5-6 and $^{d}$sùd-ur-sag (r. IV 1) could be the ugula-nimgir/nimgir é-al-la previously discussed.

The second section is also divided into two parts, each of which concludes with the clause gal-nimgir. The first of these lists four allocations for a total greater than that registered in the first section for four officials: gal-nimgir, (gal)-galla, má-$lah_4$ and nu-bànda$^{da}$. These allocations agree with what has been proposed here and should be interpreted as allocations to four nimgirs who work in the offices of the officials mentioned. Finally, the second part lists four allocations with a sum total similar to that of the first section in favour of officials identified only by their anthroponym. Of these, utu-nu-me should be identified with the uru-DU of Kullab mentioned in **4** v. V 3-4 and ur-dumu-nun with the nimgir mentioned in **12** v II 11-12; **13** r. V 6-7; VI 4; v. I 2-3; 6-7.

Let us now summarize briefly some of the salient elements which characterize the personnel who belong to the administration of the gal-nimgir.

1) The uru-DU personnel come from the various Sumerian cities, in particular from the cities of the Hexapolis. The only subordinates mentioned who have the name of a city of the Hexapolis as a characterizing element are some lú-má mentioned in the barley texts of II group and in **209**. The union of these two elements has led us to conclude that the uru-DU personnel were the "travelling personnel" of a political structure which could not have been exclusively confined to one city.
2) The presence of a nimgir within the KISAL in which the "foreign" lú-má were employed and the probable presence of another nimgir in the office of the má-

$lah_4$ testify to the connection between the nimgirs and the system for the organization of river transport.

3) The mention of nimgir-sila and alternatively of the gal-nimgir in the purchase contracts of building areas indicates a connection between the office of the gal-nimgir and the management of the streets and, more generally, of the system of road communication[49].

These considerations lead us to formulate the following hypothesis: the office of the gal-nimgir was the organizational and operative centre of the entire communications system both throughout the areas close to the city and probably also over the entire territory of the Hexapolis. From this conclusion, the extraordinary political importance of this office can be understood; it was destined by its particular position to be the nerve centre for the control of the extensive network of the close and intense political and economic relationships which seem to have existed among a group of Sumerian cities.

## 2) THE OFFICE OF THE GAL-DAM-GÀR

Among the items of **1**, two in sequence in r. II 6-III 1 concern the dam-gàr: 69 (gur) dam-gàr; [x] dam-gàr a-hu-ti[50]. These two items are the sum of all the allocations of barley of which the dam-gàr and probably also their subordinates were beneficiaries during the VII month of the last recorded year. These allocations which are mentioned in the surviving primary documentation **9-13** amount, in three cases, to 1 gur[51] and, in two cases, to 2 gur[52] for each dam-gàr and to 2 bariga and 4 bàn for

49 For a different interpretation cf. ELTS, p.237.

50 For the identification of a-hu-ti as a toponym cf. *Šuruppak*, p.36.

51 a-NI.NI dam-gàr **12** r. VII 8-9; gùr-gùr dam-gàr **11** v. VI 3-6; hur-sag-šè-mah dam-gàr **12** v. II 6-8. It should be noted that in the primary documentation **9-13** three other allocations are listed of the same amount which had been received by subordinate officials of the dam-gàr (cf. **9** v. I' 1'-4'; **11** v. II 7'-10'; **12** v. I 1-3). It is probable that these officials were themselves dam-gàr of the same rank as the three preceeding ones listed as subordinates of a high-ranking dam-gàr.

52 Here it is ad-da **11** r. VII 7-9; AK-$^{d}$sùd **11** r. I 5-7.

their subordinates[53]. This indicates that the dam-gàrs who were in the employ of the central administration were middle-to high ranking officials; some, on the basis of the parameter of payment, rank with the nimgir, others rank higher than some of the dub-sars. Some dam-gàr, of a different identity from those mentioned in the barley texts of the I group, are mentioned as beneficiaries in the barley texts of the II group[54]. The existence of dam-gàrs who receive different amounts of barley in the same texts indicates a hierarchy within this category. These we will call dam-gàr I and dam-gàr II.

In the administrative documentation of Fara, 37 dam-gàrs are mentioned altogether[55]. Of these, 19 have only the professional name dam-gàr as a characterizing element[56], 4 alternate the professional name dam-gàr with that of gal-

---

53 šubur amar-šùba dam-gàr **12** r. III 3-4; ur-dumu-zi dam-gàr **13** v. V 5-6.

54 These are: é-nu-si dam-gàr mentioned in **19** v. VIII 19-20 and **32** r. II 5-6 where he receives 1 1/2 gur and 1 gur respectively; en-nam-zu$_5$-šè dam-gàr mentioned in **29** v. IV 12-13 where he receives 1/2 gur and 2 bariga and $^{d}$sùd-anzu dam-gàr mentioned in **23** v.II 6-7 and in the parallel passages of **24** and **25** who receives 2 gur. The last-named official, $^{d}$sùd-anzu, is mentioned with a characterizing element dam-gàr only in **23-25** and receives the same quantity of barley as the other subordinates mentioned in the text who are lú-má personnel. For this reason, it is probable that he is not a dam-gàr but a lú-má in the service of the gal-dam-gàr. But the first two, é-nu-si and en-nam-zu$_5$-sè, are mentioned as dam-gàr in the texts concerning anše and lands (cf. list in note 56).

55 It is likely that these 37 officials does not exhaust the category of the dam-gàrs. In fact, it can be noted that in the first section of **139** where the beneficiaries are officials who were, for the most part, dam-gàrs some of the anthroponyms mentioned who should belong to the category of dam-gàr are not elsewhere thus described. On the other hand, it is also possible that some of the 37 officials were not dam-gàr but only subordinates of the gal-dam-gàr. An example of this is the case of $^{d}$sùd-anzu discussed in note 54.

56 a-NI.NI (**12** r. VII 8-9); abzu-ki-du$_{10}$ (**139** r. IV 3-4); AN-ur-sag (WF 63 r. II 5-6); bil$_x$-$^{d}$anzu (**82** r. V 9-10; **116** r. III 7-8; **121** v. III 11-12; in **117** v. III 5'-6' and in the parallel passage **116** r. III 7-8 this anthroponym is followed by *na-di-nu*); é-na-lu-lu (**68** r. II 4-5; **69** r. III 5-6; **74** r. III 6-7; **88** v. II 6-7; **142** r. I 1-3; **162** v. III 2-3; **177** r. IV 4-5); é-nu-nu (**121** r. IV 1-2; **124** v. II 14-15; é-nu-si (**19** v. VIII 19-20; **32** r. II 4-5; **124** r. IV 12-13; **125** v. I 2-3; **126** r. III 4-5; WF 108 r. III 4-5); é-nun-mu (**170** r. III 3-4); en-nam-zu$_5$-šè (**29** v.

dam-gàr[57] ; the remaining 14 are mentioned in the context of rather complicated sequences. These complex sequences which follow the names of some of the dam-gàrs are those of greater interest because they enable us to glimpse some of the hierarchies we are attempting to reconstruct[58] .

The sequences in question have the following schemes: a) $PN_1$ dam-gàr $PN_2$ dam-gàr; b) $PN_1$ dam-gàr $PN_2$; c) $PN_1$ $PN_2$ dam-gàr; d) $PN_1$ $PN_2$.

Sequence a) is mentioned only once in **46** r. IV 8-V 1: 20 (NI-ga) amar-tùr dam-gàr é-$^{d}$anzu dam-gàr. We have already discussed this sequence in the analysis of **46** (cf. *Šuruppak*, p.189, note 64); it could mean that either the $PN_1$ is the beneficiary of an allocation which depends on $PN_2$ or that $PN_1$ and $PN_2$ are two officials with the same rank and are both beneficiaries of the allocation. This latter interpretation is, in our opinion, more probable.

---

IV 12-13; GAR-ur-sag (**195** r. VI 5-6); KUN.KUN (**116** v. V 13-14); mes-nì-lul-le (**12** v. I 2-3; **14** r. IX 9-10; **15** v. V 6-7); mes-pà (**153** r. II 2-3); munus-á-nu-kúš (**121** r. III 5'-6'; **129** r. III 1-2; TSŠ 614 r. II 3-4); nam-mah (**115** r. IX 16-17; **124** r. IV 14-15; **125** v. I 4-5; **126** r. III 5-6; RTC 13 r. IV 4); SIG-mes-mes (**116** v. VI 6-7); $^{d}$sùd-anzu (**23** v. II 6-7; **24** r. VII 6-7; **25** r. VI 15-16); ur-utu (NTSŠ 152 r. II' 6'-7'). Finally, to these should be added KA-$^{d}$sùd-da-zi mentioned in a contract, RTC 13 r. IV 5.

57 Here we have amar-šùba (dam-gàr in **145** v. I 4-5; **162** v. II 3-4; **172** r. V 11-12;**195** r. III 3-4; NTSŠ 255 r. I 3-4; TSŠ 619 r. I 3-4; gal-dam-gàr in **124** r. III 13-14; **125** r. III 5-6; **126** r. II 6-7; **173** v. V 3-4; **174** r. V 8-9); AN-nume (dam-gàr in **88** r. II 3-4; **115** r. IX 14-15; NTSŠ 207 r. II 3-4; TSŠ 260 r. I 4-5; gal-dam-gàr in **124** r. III 9-10; **125** r. III 1-2; **126** r. II 3-4; **132** r. I 8-9; **164** r. II 1-2. This official is also described as dam-gàr a-hu-ti$^{ki}$ in TSŠ 415 r. I 1-4; TSŠ 627 r. I 8-II 2); DI-utu (dam-gàr in **116** v. II 10-11; **121** v. II 7'-8'; **122** v. I 6-7; **124** r. V 2-3; **125** r. IV 1-2, NTSŠ 207 r. III 4-5; gal-dam-gàr in **143** v. I 11-12); é-$^{d}$anzu (dam-gàr in **46** r. V 1-2; gal-dam-gàr in **116** r. I 13-14; **124** r. VIII 10-11).

58 For a preliminary discussion of the role of the dam-gàr in the administration of Fara cf. M.G.Biga, *Le attività commerciali e i commercianti nella città di Šuruppak (Fara)*, Or An 17 (1978), pp.85-105.

Sequence b) is mentioned in the following passages: ad-da dam-gàr lugal-dumu-zi (**11** r. VII 7-10)[59] ; AK-$^{d}$sùd dam-gàr ur-túl-sag (11 r.I 5-6); gúr-gúr dam-gàr unken-a (**11** v. VI 3-6), hur-sag-šè-mah dam-gàr nì-bar$_{6}$-bar$_{6}$-pa-è (**12** v. II 6-8).

Sequence c) is mentioned in the following passages: har-tu-$^{d}$sùd *ba-la* dam-gàr (**143** r. III 6-7); eden nam-šà-ta dam-gàr (**128** v. V 3-5) and MI-mud gisgal-di dam-gàr (**11** v. II 7'-10')[60] .

Sequence d) is mentioned in the following passages: har-tu-$^{d}$sùd bala$_{x}$ (**124** v. VI 9-10; **135** r. III 6-9); lu-lu lugal-dumu-zi (**124** r. IV 5-6; **125** r. IV 3-4; **139** r. II 5-6; **145** v. II 6-7); lugal-ki-dùr-du$_{10}$ lugal-dumu-zi (**139** r. III 4-5); eden nam-šà-ta (**134** v. I 5-6) and eden-si nam-šà-ta (**121** r. VIII 2-3; **136** v. IV 13-14)[61] .

The passages in sequence b) enable us to identify four officials whose subordinates were the dam-gàrs of classes I and II. These are: lugal-dumu-zi, ur-túl-sag, unken-a and nì-bar$_{6}$-bar$_{6}$-pa-è. These we will call Class A dam-gàrs. Of these, the last-mentioned is probably a dam-gàr himself; in fact, he is mentioned as a beneficiary both in a section concerning dam-gàrs (**139** r. III 3) and in a sequence together with other dam-gàrs in other texts concerning anše (**115** r. VIII 1; **121** v. I 14'; **122** r. VIII 6'; **142** v. II 2). The first-mentioned, lugal-dumu-zi, is never mentioned as the beneficiary of goods but occurs only in passages of sequence d) as the official who has as subordinates people elsewhere described as dam-gàrs (cf. lu-lu dam-gàr: **115** r. VIII 2-3; lugal-ki-dúr-du$_{10}$ dam-gàr: **126** r. II 8-9). This official is also mentioned in **171** r. II 2 as the person in charge of groups of animals. The

---

59 One ad-da is mentioned in **13** v. VI 10-12 as the official who is the superior of a beneficiary of an allocation of 2 (bariga) 4 (bàn) of barley. This latter subordinate comes from Nippur. Since no official with that anthroponym is named among the nimgir responsible for foreigners, it is possible that he is the same as the dam-gàr mentioned here. This could extend the range of the economic activities of a communitarian kind within the Hexapolis still more than has been evidenced by this study.

60 We have included in this list only those sequences in which it is certain, because of the presence of variants, that the first of the anthroponyms was also a dam-gàr.

61 We have included in this sequence only those passages where the two anthroponyms can certainly be identified with two dam-gàrs because they are mentioned both in passages in sequences b) and c) and in parallel passages in other texts.

remaining two, ur-túl-sag and unken-a, are difficult to identify. It is possible to compare ur-túl-sag with the homonymous official who in **191** r. III 1and **193** v. I 2, supplies guruš. If in these two passages reference is made to the same official, then he should be the gal-dam-gàr. In any case, these four officials, whatever their names were, must have been on one of the highest rungs of the hierarchical ladder of this office. In the passages of sequence c), it should be noted that the first anthroponym of the sequence should be regarded as a dam-gàr. In fact, both har-tu-$^{d}$sùd and eden-<si> are elsewhere mentioned as such (cf. har-tu-$^{d}$sùd dam-gàr **117** r. I 2-3; eden-si dam-gàr **123** v. I 1-2); this latter mention is parallel to a passage in **121** in sequence d) and MI-mud in **11** v. II 7' receives 1 gur like the other dam-gàrs. The second anthroponym certainly points to a dam-gàr of a higher level. *Bala* must have been the dam-gàr on whom several na-gada of the é-lugal depended (cf. *supra*, p.80; *infra*, p.119). Namšata is mentioned only in connection with eden-si while gisgal-di is not mentioned elsewhere with the characterizing element dam-gàr. *bala*, gišgal-di and nam-šà-ta can also be regarded as Class A dam-gàrs.

Summarizing we can suppose that this office had five hierarchical levels:

1. gal-dam-gàr;
2. Class A dam-gàrs;
3. Class I dam-gàrs (who receive 2 gur);
4. Class II dam-gàrs (who receive 1 gur);
5. Subordinates of the dam-gàr (who receive 2 bariga and 4 bàn).

It is probable that the high-ranking officials we have called Class A dam-gàrs were in charge of the administrative units to which the lower-ranking dam-gàrs and their subordinates belonged.

### 3) THE OFFICE OF THE GALA-MAH

One of the items of **1** (r. II 4) records the allocation of 64 (gur) for gala personnel. Like the other items examined, this is the sum total of all the allocations to the personnel of the gala-mah for the VII month. **6**, which lists these beneficiaries in detail (cf. *Šuruppak*, pp.58-64), is divided into five sections each concerning a specific category of workers. In order of mention these are: gala, šà-zu, géme-kar-gé, nu-gig and sa-HAR. The longest section must have listed about 80 people of which only 64 anthroponyms have survived. 1/2 a gur was allocated to each. These workers are described at the end of the section as dumu-dumu-gala; we have translated "(gala) workers of the gala-(mah)" (cf. *ibidem*, p.63). Thirteen of these officials are mentioned as galas in barley texts and in other types of texts[62]. On the other hand, 13 gala mentioned both in barley texts and in other text types do not appear in the surviving list of the gala in text **6**[63]. This could be due either to the lacunae in **6** or to the fact that the characterizing element gala often simply means that the persons work for the gala-mah; for example, nin-gú-gal géme-kar-gé in **11** r. I 15-16; nin-gú-gal gala in **127** r. I 8-9; **124** r. III 1-2; **125** r. II 5-6; **132** r. VII 12-13; **137** r. I 8-9. Considering the parameter of payment and since they were beneficiaries of land parcels and of allocations of anše, the galas were on the same level as the ugulas. It is, therefore, reasonable to suppose that the gala officials, like the ugulas, must have been responsible for other subordinates but the documentation does not enable us to establish their exact number or function. In fact, the other categories of workers mentioned previously as workers of the gala-mah do not seem to have a relationship of subordination to the gala officials even though they are lower-ranking as their retribution of 2 bariga and 4 bàn would seem to indicate. It is perhaps possible to consider a relationship of dependence among some of the gala on the basis of the following comparisons:

ad-da šita-kalam **132** r. II 2-3; **173** r. III 7-8; ad-da gala **115** v. V 1-2;
lum-ma šita-kalam **14** r. IX 1-2; lum-ma (gala) **6** r. VI 8';
UR.UR šita-kalam gala **14** r. VII 18-20; UR.UR is never mentioned as gala;
šita-kalam (gala) **6** r. IV 2'.

---

62 These are: á-nu-kúš mentioned in **115** r. III 1-2 (this corresponds to the gala mentioned in **6** r. II 6'); AN-úr-šè in NTSŠ **118** r. V 1-2 (**6** r. I 6'); AŠ-mud in **139** v. I 4-5 (**6** r. V 4'); du$_{6}$-du$_{6}$ in **87** r. II 3-4 (**6** r. V 6'); é-nu-si **9** r. I' 1' (**6** r. VI 6'); é-na-lu-lu **9** r. I' 3' (**6** r. III 2'); é-pirig in TSŠ 248 r. II 5-6 (**6** r. I 1); lugal-AN-diri **9** r. I' 4' (**6** r. IV 9'); lu-lu **9** r. II' 3' (**6** r. I 3'); NI-gi$_{4}$-a **9** r. II' 4' (**6** r. I 4'); nin-bàd **9** r. II' 1'-2' (**6** r. III 6'); šita-kalam in **14** r. VII 19-20 (**6** r. IV 2'); zadim-si **9** r. I' 2' (**6** r. V 11').

63 These are: a-RI-ti (**115** r. IX 1-2); ad-da (**115** v. IV 1-2); en-pa-è (**115** r. X 12-13); gúr-gúr (WF 35 r. V 9-10); KA.<KA>.Ú (**87** v. I 5-II 1; **213** r. I 1-2); KA.Ú-za$_{7}$ (**115** r. VII 11-12); kas$_{4}$-KAB-ta (NSRJ 3 v. II 4-5); kin-nir-<si> (**115** r. II 2-5; **137** r. IV 7-8); munus-lú-nu-šè (**13** v. II 8-9); nam-tur (**213** r. I 3); sag-nar (WF 30 r. IV 3-4); šakan-[ ] (**18** v. IV 1-2); ur-tur (WF 35 v. I 4-5).

If, on the one hand, we cannot be certain that ad-da and lum-ma gala should be identified with the homonyms mentioned in **132** and **14**, on the other, there are no differentiated parameters of payment among the gala as emerges from **6** where both lum-ma and šita-kalam are mentioned.

The second group listed in **6** (r. II 1-IV 5) is more numerous; it is that of the géme-kar-gé. This group seems to contain, in addition to the géme-kar-gé strictly speaking, the šim-mú and the har-tu[64] who probably had some connection with the work of the former. The names of the workers in question are followed by a characterizing element, absent in the section concerning the gala. The element is usually the name of an official. Among these, igi-gùn is mentioned several times. This official is not present as a beneficiary in the list of the géme-kar-gé in **6** but is mentioned as the official whose subordinate is géme-kar-gé sal-la (sal-la igi-gùn: **6** v. II 12-13). Since in the corresponding item in **11** r. VII 11-13 igi-gùn is mentioned as the géme-kar-gé of whom sal-la is a subordinate (sal-la igi-gùn géme-kar-gé), we must regard igi-gùn as a high-ranking official in this category.

The sal-la mentioned in **6** v. I 13-14 must have had a similar function with regard to the ten šà-zu listed in the second section of **6** (v. I 1-2). It has proved impossible to identify any hierarchy among the nu-gig of the IV section of **6** (v. V 1-6) who are mentioned without any characterizing element.

It has been noted that there is a relationship between the gala, the géme-kar-gé, the sa-HAR, the nar and the SAL.UŠ (cf. *Šuruppak*, pp.41, 244-245) on the basis of the following variants:

AN-úr-šè gala NTSŠ 118 r. V 1-2; AN-úr-sè nar unug$^{ki}$ **4** r. IV 10-12;
igi-gùn sa-HAR **14** r. II 2-3; igi-gùn géme-kar-gé **11** r. VII 5-6;
NI.NI sa-HAR **181** v. I 6-7; **182** r. II 6-7; NI.NI nar **184** v. II 4-5;
nin-ni-gi$_4$ géme-kar-gé pa$_4$-NÁM **11** r. I 12-14; nin-ni-gi$_4$ nar$_x$ pa$_4$-NÁM **6** v. III 5;
ur-lamma sa-HAR **74** r. V 3-4; ur-lamma nar **68** r. IV 5-6; **70** r. I 1-2; **72** v. I 1-2.

The interchange in these passages establishes an equivalence between the professions of sa-HAR, géme-kar-gé and nar and closely relates the activity of the subordinates of the gala-mah to that of the subordinates of some im-rus of the é-gal

64 For the meaning "slave, servant" for this term cf. P.Steinkeller, *Akkad*, p.121, no.38.

where nar and SAL.UŠ are mentioned: these are the im-rus of DI-utu and $^{d}$sùd-ur-sag ugula lú-ad.

If, on the one hand, the documentation of Fara enables us to establish to what sector of the administration the personnel mentioned belongs, on the other, it does not provide us with any element to understand the role which this personnel must have played. I.J.Gelb in his article, *Homo Ludens in Early Mesopotamia*, in Festschrift A.Salonen, StOr 46, pp.43-76, notes the close connection between the gala, nar, muš-lah$_4$ and the UD.DA.TUŠ[65] both in the Ur III texts and in the Sargonic and pre-Sargonic texts relating to the same activity. In these texts, the gala seems to have had many functions: cantor, wailer, lamenter, liturgist, psalmist. The meaning proposed by Gelb for the term gala is "homosexual or pederast" since the gala are often connected with the géme thus rejecting the rendering "eunuch" proposed by other scholars (cf. *ibidem*, pp.69-72)[66] . In Gelb's study, the level of the galas varies greatly both in the documents of pre-Sargonic Lagash and in those of Ur III; from the plethora of galas (who can also be bought as the pre-Sargonic contracts testify cf. *ibidem*, pp.65-66) who attend the funeral of Baranamtarra, wife of Lugalanda, to the well-off gala who possess lands and goods. While the connection between gala and women has been established in the documentation of Fara like that with the nar, sa-HAR and SAL.UŠ, all the gala appear to be middle- to high-ranking officials similar to the ugulas. All of them together with the géme-kar-gé, nu-gig, sa-HAR and šà-zu are subordinates of the gala-mah and form part of the organization of the é-gal. It cannot, however, be excluded that personnel of a much lower level than the géme-kar-gé, the nu-gig and the šà-zu could have been the subordinates of the gala. But it has not been possible to ascertain this because the personnel at a lower level than the last-mentioned workers with the single exception of the lú-ri-ri-ga of **1** and of the nu-su personnel of the nimgirs are never mentioned as beneficiaries in the administrative documentation from Fara.

---

65 The term gìr-šè-ga (from the Akkadian *girsequ*) which indicates this personnel collectively (cf. *Homo Ludens*, p.55) should be linked to the lú-ad personnel mentioned in the Fara texts which groups nar, SAL.UŠ etc.; we have rendered these generically as court personnel (cf. *Šuruppak*, pp.34, 42)

66 I.J.Gelb notes that from the documentation some of the gala are married with children (cf. *Homo Ludens*, p.67-69).

4) THE OFFICE OF THE É-GÉME

The office of the é-géme seems to have played a vital role in the administrative structure of Šuruppak. In the analysis and commentary on the barley texts of the III group **38-40** (cf. *Šuruppak*, p.178) we posited the existence of an office which coordinated the two most important administrative centres. These texts, all of which come from the site XVII c,d, record considerable quantities of barley for which a small group of officials were responsible. These have been identified only through their anthroponym. By means of a series of comparisons, it has been possible to identify these officials as dub-sars. Some of them are mentioned in the barley texts of the I and II groups; we know that these documents are general summary documents from two different administrative centres. This fact suggested to us the idea that these dub-sars had a role both of coordination and control between these centres and that in this capacity they formed part of an office directly connected with the highest authority of the state. Among the centres mentioned in the administrative documentation of Fara, the é-géme is the office which seems to possess these characteristics. In fact, this office is mentioned repeatedly in all types of texts from those regarding the allocations of goods (barley, grain, beverages, copper, anše, parcels of land) to those relative to personnel. The personnel connected with this office are all middle- to high-ranking officials; dub-sars, engars and ugulas. Some mentions of officials who belong to this office contain variants which enable us to clarify certain aspects of the role of the é-géme.

1) AN-nu-me engar é-géme (**135** v. VI 2-3); AN-nu-me engar dumu-zi (CT 50, 5 r. IV 5-6); AN-nu-me engar énsi-GAR (**11** r. V 5-6).
2) amar-tùr ugula é-géme (**46** r. III 2-3); amar-šùba nagar amar-tùr ugula (**151** r. I 4-6); amar-šùba nagar $sa_{12}$-$du_5$ (**37** v. II' 1'-3').
3) ku-li é-géme (**116** v. I 15-16); ku-li ur-dumu-zi (**171** r. VII 13-14).
4) lam-ma é-géme (TSŠ 308 r. II 6'-7'): lam-ma sanga-GAR (NTSŠ 211 v. II 4); lam-ma ur-dumu-zi (**29** r. IV 14-15).
5) lum-ma dub-sar é-géme (**121** v. IV 6-8; **122** v. IV 1-3); lum-ma dub-sar-anše $sa_{12}$-$du_5$ (**7** v. I 1-3); lum-ma énsi-GAR (TSŠ 302 v. VI 5).
6) $^{d}$sùd-ur-sag engar é-géme (**116** v. VI 3-4); $^{d}$sùd-ur-sag engar amar-nam-nir ugula (énsi-GAR) (**13** v. VI 12-14); $^{d}$sùd-ur-sag engar dumu-dumu (**116** r. III 5).

From this list of variants the following can be deduced:

a) The office of the é-géme is so closely connected to the énsi-GAR that the two qualifications should be regarded as practically synonymous (cf. 1, 5 and 6);

b) The $sa_{12}$-$du_5$ is one of the officials in charge of the é-géme (cf. 2 and 5)[67];

c) The sanga-GAR is probably another official of the é-géme (cf. 4).

The interchange <ur>-dumu-zi / é-géme which can be seen in 1), 2) and 3) is more complex to interpret. This anthroponym is widespread in the onomasticon of Fara; at least three high-ranking officials are characterized by this anthroponym. They are: ur-dumu-zi ${}^{d}$en-líl-pà/nu-bànda[68]; ur-dumu-zi dub-sar and ur-dumu-zi énsi-GAR. It should be noted that ur-dumu-zi énsi-GAR and ur-dumu-zi dub-sar are mentioned contemporaneously in the same text (**143** r. IV 7-8; r. VI 6-7); for this reason they must have been different persons. In addition, a comparison between the following interchanges:

${}^{d}$sùd-anzu ur-dumu-zi dub-sar (**14** r. V 14-15)
${}^{d}$sùd-anzu ur-dumu-zi (**35** v. IV 3-4)
${}^{d}$sùd-anzu dumu-zi (TSŠ 536 v.II 3-4)
${}^{d}$sùd-anzu ${}^{d}$en-líl-pà (**120** v. I 2-3)
ur-dumu-zi ${}^{d}$en-líl-pà (**23** v. II 11-12)

leads us to the conclusion that ur-dumu-zi, the subordinate of ${}^{d}$en-líl-pà, must have been the same person as the homonymous dub-sar[69].

---

67 It should be remembered that this official should probably be identified with the ur-${}^{d}$lamma (cf. *Šuruppak*, p.138).

68 For the identification of ${}^{d}$en-lìl-pà with the nu-bànda of the KISAL cf. *infra*, p.114.

69 In **15** v. III 11-IV 1 an ur-dumu-zi dub-sar $pa_4$-${}^{d}$anzu is mentioned but the fact that this dub-sar is a subordinate of $pa_4$-${}^{d}$anzu need not contradict the preceding deduction. In fact, analysing the mentions of other subordinates of $pa_4$-${}^{d}$anzu (cf. **171** r. V 4'-5'; **195** r. VI 13-14: lum-ma $pa_4$-${}^{d}$anzu; **37** r. II' 7'-8': utu-šita $pa_4$-${}^{d}$anzu) we note that these officials are described in other texts as dub-sar (cf. lum-ma dub-sar é-géme/anše $sa_{12}$-$du_5$: **121** v. IV 6-8; **122** v. IV 1-2; **7** v. I 3-4; utu-šita dub-sar: **116** r. I 7-8; **117** v I 7'-8'; **146** r. III 4-5; **157** r. I 7-8; TSŠ 70 r. II 2-3). This observation makes the identification of $pa_4$-${}^{d}$anzu with dub-sar-mah, namely, the head of a corporation, possible. In any case, all the dub-sar, whoever they were and wherever they were employed, belonged to such a corporation.

Having identified ur-dumu-zi dub-sar as the official who was the subordinate of the nu-bànda $^{d}$en-lìl-pà, we can, by exclusion, identify the ur-dumu-zi who alternates with é-géme in 1), 2) and 3) with ur-dumu-zi énsi-GAR. This identification fits in well with what we said in a) above, namely, that the office of the é-géme depended directly on the énsi-GAR-gal as did the officials who worked there. In the case of the ur-dumu-zi in question, one could, on the basis of the interchange in 4) perhaps recognize one of the highest-ranking officials, that is, the sanga-GAR. Within the limits of these identifications, often hypothetical, of the high-ranking officials of the administration of Šuruppak, the existence and the role of the é-géme at the apex of the political and administrative organization of Šuruppak appears to be quite clear.

Because of the limits of the documentation, we cannot make precise affirmations on the relationships which the sanga-GAR and the $sa_{12}$-$du_5$ must have had with this office. The sanga-GAR, as appears from the documentation, had as subordinates dub-sar, géme-kar-gé, maškim, SAL.UŠ, šu-i and $tigi_x$-di and about ten other officials whose profession is not specified[70]. These were the recipients of barley in the texts of I and the II group. The $sa_{12}$-$du_5$ had as subordinates dub-sar, maškim, nagar and šu-i and less than ten other officials whose profession is not specified[71] and who were paid in the barley texts of both the I and the II group. But

70 The dub-sar sanga-GAR are: amar-kù (**10** v. II 6-7); $^{d}$sùd-anzu (**10** r. VI 2'-4'); šubur (TSŠ 430 r. III 4'-5') and zà-ta (**10** v. V 1-2). The géme-kar-gé sanga-GAR nin-gú-gal is mentioned in **11** r. I 15-II 1. The maškim sanga-GAR AK is mentioned in TSŠ 627 r. III 7-8. The SAL.UŠ amar-kù is mentioned in **29** v. III 15-17; **115** r. I 9-11 and in the parallel texts, **121** r. VIII 9-10. The šu-i sanga-GAR utu-ur-sag is mentioned in WF 136 r. II 4-6. en-nam-$zu_5$-šè $tigi_x$-di sanga-GAR is mentioned in **7** v. II 5-6. This latter official is probably a dub-sar $tigi_x$-di (cf. *Šuruppak*, p.66). The workers whose profession is not specified are DI-utu and subordinates of $^{d}$sùd-nu-me (**171** r. VIII 10-12; **187** v. II 9-10); KA-$^{giš}$gigir (TSŠ 618 r. I 2'-3'); lam-ma (**153** v. II 5-6); mes-nu-sig (**127** r. III 9-10; MI+ZA (**28** r. III 13-14); munus-á-nu-kúš (**23** r. VI 14); nin-ur-sag (WF 108 v. I 1-2); $pa_4$-ur-sag (TSŠ 47 r. II' 3'-4') and sag-TAR (TSŠ 614 r. I 5-6).

71 The dub-sar $sa_{12}$-$du_5$ is lum-ma (**7** v. I 3-5): the maškim $sa_{12}$-$du_5$ AN-nu-me (**14** v. V 19-20; **17** v. I 7-8; **18** v. V 2-3) and ad-da (**115** v. I 10-12); the nagar $sa_{12}$-$du_5$ amar-šùba (**37** v. II' 9'-10'); the šu-i $^{d}$sùd-à-mah (**12** r. III 12-IV 1; **36** r. IV 1'-3'). The other officials are: a-nu-nu (**7** r. III 1-2); a-gestin (NTSŠ 154 r. III 2-3); gúr-gúr (**11** v. IX 6-7; **195** v. II 4-5);

whatever the relationship between these high-ranking officials and the office of the é-géme were, the vast majority of their subordinates must have belonged to this office.

We can conclude by stating that the é-géme was probably the operational office of the highest authority of the state, namely, of the énsi. To it must have belonged, in some way, all the dub-sars, all six engar-énsi/é-géme[72] and at least three ugula-énsi/é-géme[73], that is, all the key officials of the organizational system.

---

hur-sag-šè-mah (**62** r. II 2-3); KA-ni-zi (**36** r. VI 6-7; **187** v. II 2-3). This latter individual should be identified with the homonymous engar ur-$^{d}$lamma mentioned in **27** r. I 14-16. Then there is ur-ab-ba$_6$ (**27** r. I 1-3, probably a lú-má) and ur-$^{d}$tu (**94** r. III 6-7).

72 In addition to AN-nu-me and $^{d}$sùd-ur-sag, there are ur-NI, lugal-KA.KAL and é-pirig-gal mentioned in **11** r. V 3-10 and nì-kur-ra mentioned in **37** r. IV' 4'-6'.

73 These are: amar-nam-nir mentioned as ugula-énsi (cf. *Šuruppak*, p.92), amar-šùba and amar-tùr mentioned as ugula-é-géme (**46** r. II 8-III 2). All these officials are mentioned in sequence both in **188** r. IV 1-3 and **191** r. II 5-7 as well as in **172** r. V 11-13.

## § 2. The Administration of the é-uru

The officials and their subordinates who were paid in the II group of the barley texts must have belonged to the administrative centre of the é-uru. The vast majority of these subordinates were:

a) the lú-má and addir$_x$ who belonged to the office of the KISAL;

b) the na-gada, sipa and utul who belonged to the breeding centres;

c) the craftsmen who belonged to the offices of the corporation heads;

d) the šu-ku$_6$ and other subordinates who belonged to the office of the enku.

### 1) The office of the KISAL

The existence of this office was evidenced in the analysis of the guruš texts in the chapter I. We identified the officials, mentioned in the first five groups of **187**, essentially as ugulas and as those who were entrusted with the supervision of the personnel. Many of the ugulas of **187**, are mentioned in **23** and in the parallel texts **24** and **25**; these documents are described in their colophons as dub-lú-má,"registers of the personnel (in charge of) the ships". The remaining ugulas even though they are not mentioned in these texts are described in other documents as lú-má or addir$_x$. Consequently, we can conclude that these ugulas were in charge of the lú-má personnel. Of the 300 members of the above-mentioned five groups, 120, those of the first and third groups, seem to to have belonged to an administrative centre headed by the ugula of the énsi-GAR, amar-nam-nir; while, the remaining 180, listed in the second, fourth and fifth groups, seem to have belonged to the administrative centre of the KISAL. The official in charge of this latter centre was the nu-bànda whom we can almost certainly identify with Enlil-pa. This identification arises from a comparison of the following passages:

a) ur-$^d$sùd ugula $^d$en-líl-pà (**23** r. VII 3-5); ur-$^d$sùd nu-bànda (**187** r. II 5-6); ur-$^d$sùd KISAL (NTSŠ 92 r. III 9-10).

b) ur-dumu-zi $^d$en-líl-pà (**23** v. II 11-12); ur-dumu-zi nu-bànda (**123** v. V 6-7;**128** r. II 1-2).

c) eden-si ugula (**24** r. VIII 10-12); eden-si nu-bànda (**23** v. IV 3-4)

d) é-la-lum$_x$ $^d$en-líl-pà (**116** r. IV 20-21); úr-NI é-la-lum$_x$ (**115** r .VIII 6-7); úr-NI KISAL (**82** r. II 1-2; **128** v. V 10-11; **138** r. IV 3-4)

If, in fact, the nu-bànda $^{d}$en-líl-pà is the official in charge of the KISAL then not only do ugulas and their lú-má belong to this centre but also the engars mentioned in TSŠ 522 r. I 3-6 who are subordinates of $^{d}$en-líl-pà (cf. *Šuruppak*, p.100). These Class B engars, mentioned in the barley texts of the II group, must have been in charge of the barley allocated to the lú-má workers. To these should be added é-la-lum$_{x}$, a Class B engar mentioned in the fourth section of **29** as a subordinate of $^{d}$en-lìl-pà. In addition, the nimgir nin-<en>-kalam-<ma>, described as nimgir KISAL in **16** v. II 10-11 and WF 42 r. III 7-IV 1 and simply as lú-KISAL a subordinate of $^{d}$en-lìl-pà in TSŠ 522 r. I 1-2, is mentioned as belonging to the KISAL. This official should be identified with the official, a subordinate of the gal-nimgir, who belongs to the office of the nu-bànda mentioned in NTSŠ 118 v. I 5. The significance of the presence of this official within the KISAL is not immediately evident but it should be linked to the relationship which existed between the uru-DU personnel in the service of the nimgir and the lú-má uru-kas$_{4}$ personnel whom we believe to have been in the service of the nu-bànda in the KISAL. The feature these two categories of subordinates have in common is that of being "foreign" travelling personnel hailing from other cities of the Hexapolis (cf. *Šuruppak*, pp.11-21 and 54). Since this "foreign" personnel is under the jurisdiction of the nimgirs, it is therefore probable that the nimgir-KISAL was the nimgir, stationed in the KISAL, who was in charge of the "foreign" lú-má. The mention of such a large number of personnel employed in river transportation can only indicate that trade and the consequent transport of goods must have been one of the principal activities of Šuruppak, at least in the period of these texts. It is therefore probable that the task of the KISAL was that of the coordination and organization of a large part of the river transportation system. The other part of the system was managed, as we have already seen above, by the énsi directly through the office of the é-géme[74] .

---

[74] The professions gal-KISAL, lú-KISAL and KISAL occur in almost all the archaic lexical lists (cf. ZATU, *sub voce* 295; UET 2, 264 r. I' 2'; 299 I 3'; MSL XII, p.10, n.23; p.15, n.11). Professional names linked to the KISAL also recur in the administrative texts of Uruk III and Girsu ED III b and Early Sargonic Umma.

### 3) THE CATTLE BREEDING CENTRES

About thirty texts in the administrative documentation of Fara refer to sheep and small cattle and there are about ten texts concerning wool (cf. ***Šuruppak***, p.1-2). No element emerges from the texts which would indicate that the cattle recorded were allocated or that it was a question of endowments even though there is some evidence to suppose, like the findspot, the officials mentioned etc., that this was true in some cases. The great majority of the texts are lists containing few items which refer to small numbers of beasts. There are, however, some exceptions: WF 125 has two items listing about 1,050 udu-nita as well as 150 other dah, "additions", of which ur-ba-ba na-gada is in charge; then there are WF 127, 131, TSŠ 906, 929, CT 50, 25; these contain more items for a sum total, in each text, of a few hundred animals. The documents have some reciprocal correspondences even if not to the same extent as other categories of documents (like the barley texts and texts concerning fields, anše, dumu-dumu and guruš personnel). The few indications present in this documentation do not enable us to chart the organizational system which underpinned this activity nor to understand the role and importance the breeding of animals had in the economy of Fara nor even to estimate approximately the number of persons employed in this activity. But the mentions in the documentation concerning barley, fields, anše and guruš indicate the presence of personnel employed in this activity which is much more numerous that what the surviving texts concerning cattle and wool would lead us to think.

This personnel depended on the central administration and was organized according to the hierarchical and bureaucratic canons already encountered regarding the other workers. In addition, we learn from the texts concerning anše that a considerable number of equids were allocated to different officials who were beneficiaries of allotment fields in order to carry out agricultural work. Since the arable land granted for sustenance was only a small fraction of the state lands, we must suppose that the number of equids employed both in agricultural work and in transport was much greater than that documented in the anše texts. These two considerations lead us to suppose that animal breeding was more highly developed than appears from the few texts concerning small animals and wool which have survived. It is probable that the tablets in question do not come from the archives of the organized breeding centres whose summary accounts must have been preserved in a different place than that from which the greater part of the administrative documentation of the D.O.G. came. It is likely that they were records of particular transactions some of which were supposed in Chapter II §. 2

The first text which indicates the existence of centres connected with the breeding of animals is **210**. In the colophon, three groups of 5, 6 and 3 na-gada are listed; they belong to three different centres. In fact, the first group of na-gada is described as $gu_4$-gur-SI whose meaning is uncertain[75]. But the mention of the two other centres both in the text and in the colophon to which other na-gada belong suggests that the term, even if it is probably in abbreviated form, must indicate a centre for the breeding of animals.

KA-zi[76], this anthroponym is not mentioned elsewhere with the description na-gada.

AN-nu-me is the na-gada mentioned in **68** v. IV 15-V 1 and **76** v. III 9-10. From a comparison with parallel passages in **68** v.IV 15 and **72** v. III 9-10, we learn that he is a subordinate of $^{d}$sùd-anzu who is probably the IB <PA> $^{d}$sùd mentioned in many texts concerning anše and fields[77].

nì-$zu_5$-kur-šè is the na-gada mentioned in **82** v. II 9-III 1; perhaps he should be identified with a subordinate of ur-dumu-zi[78].

lú-$su_{13}$ is the na-gada mentioned in **92** r. II 1-2; **133** r. II 2'-3' and **136** v. III 9'-10'. In TSŠ 499 r. I 1-3 he is the person in charge of 84 $kir_{11}$.

dumu-$^{d}$anzu is the na-gada mentioned in **133** r. III 9'-10' where he precedes DI-utu na-gada. In **134** r. III 3-4 and in the barley text **19** v. I 17-18 he is

---

75 This term could have different meanings according to the order of the signs (for the meaning of $gu_4$-gur and dumu-$gu_4$-gur cf. H.Waetzold, UNT, p.79). The proposed order makes the reading $gu_4$-gur-má possible; the meaning would thus be "handlers of cattle in charge of the oxen used to tow the boats".

76 This anthroponym is certainly an abbreviated form both of KA-ni-zi and of KA-zi-da. For this reason, it is probable that the complete name is KA-ni-zi-da (cf. SRJ 6 v. I 8-9: KA-zi-da engar-UŠ; NSRJ 3 v. II 4-5: KA-ni-zi engar-UŠ; **10** r. II 3-5: KA-ni-zi engar-UŠ ur-$^{d}$tu).

77 Cf. **84** r. II 6-7; **93** r. II 4-5; **94** r. IV 9-10; **124** r. IV 8-9; **125** r. IV 5-6; **126** r. III 10-11; **128** v. IV 6-7; **129** r. II 6-7; **134** v. V 11-12. The same official in **89** v. III 1-3 is mentioned in the sequence AN-nu-me $^{d}$sùd-anzu $si_4$-na.

78 Cf. **68** r. IV 1-2; **70** r. I 1-3; **86** r. III 2; **125** v. III 9-10.

mentioned as the superior of lu-lu. This latter anthroponym is probably an abbreviation of mes-lu-lu na-gada mentioned in **16** r. I 7-8 and in HHS 3,1 r. V 4. The na-gada dumu-$^{d}$anzu together with mes-lu-lu, DI-utu, ad-da and ur-$^{d}$gù-là are the components of the fourteenth group of officials who provide men for conscription (cf. *supra*, p.59).

Beside the na-gada of our text, a high-ranking official is mentioned in connection with a $gu_4$-gur-SI; this is $^{d}$sùd-ur-sag engar $gu_4$-gur-SI mentioned in **146** r. II 5-6. The same official is mentioned in **116** r. II 5-6 with the description engar-dumu-dumu and as engar é-géme in v. VI 3-5 of the same text. Thus, he should be identified with the engar who is the direct subordinate of amar-nam-nir already mentioned as ugula énsi-GAR in **13** r. VI 11-14[79].

From the mention of $gu_4$-gur-SI subordinates and officials, we can conclude that these like ad-da, DI-utu, mes-lu-lu and perhaps ur-$^{d}$gù-là were probably connected, on the one hand, with a temple-like administration $^{d}$sùd (cf. *infra*, p.120-121) and, on the other, with the office of the é-géme. Since these officials of the $^{d}$sùd centre received allocations of barley in the texts of the II group, this means that this centre must have been under the direct control of the énsi and of the office of the é-géme.

The second centre mentioned in **210** is the é-lugal. To this centre belonged, as can be seen from the colophon, the six na-gada mentioned. The five, whose anthroponyms have survived, are mentioned elsewhere in the documentation of Fara:

zà-ta is a na-gada mentioned in **135** v. VII 5-6.

ur-sipa is a na-gada whose subordinate is munus-á-nu-kúš (CT 50, 25 r. III' 2'-4').

en-nu-kur-šè is a na-gada mentioned in **68** v. V 2-3; **72** v.I V 1-2; **92** r. II 3-4; **121** r. IV 14-15; **123** v. III 2'-3'; TSŠ 89 v. III 1-2. This na-gada is the superior both of šubur (**115** r. V 2) and AN-úr-sè (**115** r. VII 16-18).

---

79 TSŠ 522 mentions in r. II 5-9 a group of four engars: mes-nu-sè, lam-ma, ad-da and šeš-ni. The qualification of these engars is given in r. II 9 but the reading of the sign copied by R.Jestin presents some difficulty. In *Šuruppak*, p.100 we proposed the reading $gu_4$-gur for that sign. This would imply that four other Class B engars were connected with this centre but they must have been subordinates of $^{d}$sùd-ur-sag or of lower rank. But the reading engar-$addir_x$ cannot be excluded.

ba-zi is a na-gada mentioned in **46** r. V 7-8; **73** v. II 5-6; **132** r. VI 3-4; **134** r. IV 6-7. The mention in **46** indicates that he is a middle-to high-ranking official on the same level as the other officials mentioned in that text (cf. *Šuruppak*, p.189).

unken-a is a na-gada mentioned in **177** r. I 1-2. From the parallel passage, **174** r. III 5-6, we learn that this anthroponym is an abbreviation of nin-unken-a, the na-gada mentioned in **29** v. IV 19-20; **143** v. I 5-6; **164** r. I 4-5[80].

From a comparison with a passage in **37** both $^{d}$sùd-anzu and NI.NI belong to the é-lugal. The former is difficult to understand since he is not mentioned elsewhere as a na-gada or sipa; the latter is the na-gada *ba-la*/*bala*$_x$ mentioned in **46** r. V 5-6; **139** v. VI 3-5; **158** r. II 2-4. Another official of the é-lugal connected with the cult aspect is mes-u$_4$-ba ì-du$_8$ é-lugal mentioned in **115** v. V 13-15; **121** v. II' 13'-14'. He recurs only as ì-du$_8$ in WF 121 r. IV 4-5 and is perhaps to be identified with mes-u$_4$-ba dumu-èš in **164** v. I 6-7[81].

---

80 The dam-gàr gúr-gúr is a subordinate of an unken-a in **11** v. VI 4-6 (cf. also **116** v. II 15-16; **139** r. III 8-9) whom we have identified as a Class A dam-gàr. We have, also, established that unken-a na-gada é-lugal is a subordinate of *ba-la* dam-gàr (cf. *Šuruppak*, 175-176). It is possible that the Class A dam-gàr unken-a coincides with this na-gada. In this way we have established a possible relationship between officials employed in the breeding of animals and the activity of the dam-gàrs.

81 In the documentation of Fara, besides ì-du$_8$ é-lugal, the following "guardians of the door" are mentioned: ba-za ì-du$_8$ $^{d}$dumu-zi in WF 33 r. V 6-8; DU.LUL ì-du$_8$ é-ama in **13** r. I 1-4; utu-šita ì-du$_8$ PA.PA in **115** v. VI 8-9; this latter is mentioned only as ì-du$_8$ in **121** v.II 16'-17' and **122** v.II 1-2. Other anthroponyms followed by the element ì-du$_8$ without further characterization are: ad-da (cf.**116** v. III 11-12; **117** v. III 7'-8'), é-zi-pa-è (cf. **35** v. II 6-7), nin-$^{d}$anzu (cf. WF 63 r. I 4-5), šubur (cf. **19** v. IV 3-4; **21** v. III' 3'-4'; **30** v. III 12'-13'), ur-$^{d}$sùd (cf. MVN 10, 86 r. III 6-7). It is possible that the characterizing element $^{d}$gibil$_6$, with which é-zi-pa-è is mentioned in many texts concerning fields, asses and carts, is an abbreviation of ì-du$_8$ $^{d}$gibil$_6$. A similar consideration can be made for šubur followed in some cases by the divine element $^{d}$nam-URUxSIG$_7$ (cf. **116** r. V 4-5; **117** v. IV 6-7; **118** r. I 2'-3'; **172** r. VIII 8-9). An anthroponym rarely mentioned, nin-$^{d}$anzu, is followed by IB in **195** v. I 13-II 1. This IB could be identified with the ì-du$_8$ mentioned previously because the two professions refer to the same sphere of activity.

Other officials have lugal as a characterizing element:

1) du$_{11}$-ga-ni lugal (**19** r. VI 3-4; **28** r. II 6-8). The official should probably be identified with the na-gada mentioned in **68** v. IV 11-12 and **72** v. III 5-6.
2) lam-ma lugal (**19** v. II 7-8). It is possible that this official was the same as the homonymous subordinate of mes-u$_4$-ba (cf. **7** r. II 7-8) and UR.UR (cf. **127** v. IV 7-8)[82].
3) eden-aš$_8$ lugal (TSŠ 503 r.II 3-4). This anthroponym is mentioned nowhere else in the documentation of Fara but we cannot exclude that it is a variant of eden-AŠ, an official of whom é-na and ku-li are subordinates (cf.**12** r. I 7; 9).
4) AB.GAR.SI zimbir$^{ki}$ lugal (TSŠ 881 r. VI 11'-12'). He is not mentioned elsewhere.
5) kur$_4$-da unug$^{ki}$ lugal (TSŠ 369 r. II 7-8). He is probably a lú-má. An unnamed ugula má-gur$_8$ is a subordinate of this lugal and is mentioned in the same text in r. II 3-4.
6) Another unnamed maškim lugal a-hu-ti[83] is mentioned in CT 50, 15 r. II 2-4.

What seems to emerge from all these mentions is that the é-lugal had, on the one hand, personnel employed in the breeding of animals and, on the other, personnel connected with the religious sphere. Consequently in the documentation of Fara these two activities seem to be related.

The third centre mentioned in **210** in which three na-gada are employed is called é-gu$_4$, literally, "the house of oxen", that is, an organizational centre for large animals. The two surviving anthroponyms are:

1) na-ni-<a>, a na-gada mentioned in an anše text **121** v.VI 5'-6' and in the parallel passage **122** v.VI 7-8. This official has na-gada šà-uru$^?$ as a characterizing element in the latter text.

---

82 Both of these persons are reciprocally related and probably should be connected with the breeding of animals (cf. *Šuruppak*, p.421).

83 a-hu-ti is in this case a toponym (cf. AN-nu-me dam-gàr a-hu-ti$^{ki}$ TSŠ 627; dam-gàr a-hu-ti **1** r. I 1-2) within perhaps the administrative jurisdiction of Šuruppak. Neverhless, this toponym seems do not connected to the term lugal but to verbal form mu-gi$_4$-a that follows it in the text. The passage of CT 50, 15 r. II 1-v. I 1: 2 túg / maškim / lugal / a-hu-ti / mu-gi$_4$-a / mes-lú-nu-šè / mu-da-DU, is perhaps to be translated "2 cloths, that the maškim of the lugal has brought from Ahuti, has delivered by Meslunushe".

2) pa-bil$_x$-ga is another na-gada mentioned in **132** v.IV 5-6; **137** r.II 1-2 and **177** r.II 4-5.

There is only one other mention of an official who belongs to the é-gu$_4$. This is dumu-nun-šita nu-kiri$_6$ é-gu$_4$ mentioned in **116** v.IV 4-6; he appears only as nu-kiri$_6$ in **124** v.IV 9-10. It is possible that AN.URUDU-si mentioned as ugula lú-gu$_4$ in TSŠ 424 v.II 2-3 and only as lú-gu$_4$ in **128** r.III 5-6 belonged to this centre just as lú-bára-du$_{10}$ sipa-gu$_4$ (cf. **140** v.II 5-6). However, the real importance of this centre escapes us and, with the exception of **211**, it is rarely mentioned in the texts of Fara.

In addition to the centres mentioned in **211**, others of perhaps still greater importance concern the breeding of animals. These centres appear to be temple organizations connected with the worship of various divinities like $^{d}$sùd, $^{d}$gibil, kin-nir etc (cf. *Šuruppak*, p.176). The colophons of some texts concerning anše, like **130** and **146**, contain the clause anše $^{d}$sùd or anše-apin $^{d}$sùd (cf. *ibidem*, p.356-357) while the colophon of **170** has the abbreviated formula sur$_x$-anše AN (for the interchange AN/$^{d}$sùd cf. *ibidem*, p.211) which can be rendered "teams of asses for the goddess Sud".

On the basis of the documentation, a certain number of officials belong to the centre identified by the name of divinities.

**1) The $^{d}$sùd Centre**

a) na-gada or sipa officials:

<u>abzu-ta-mud</u>, who generally appears in the abbreviated forms abzu-mud, ab-ta-mud and ab-mud, is mentioned as a sipa AN/$^{d}$sùd in the texts concerning fields (**84** v.I 5-6), anše (**127** r.III 3-4; **128** r.II 8-9; **137** r.II 15-16) and carts (**176** r.IV 3-4). He is mentioned as na-gada in **68** v. II 5-6; **115** r. II 10-11; 117 r. III 4-5; **122** r. VII 7'-8'[84].

---

84 The sequence é-nanna šeš ab-mud nu-bànda (**18** v. IV 5-8) could provide the key for reading the term gu$_4$-gur-SI. In fact, the nu-bànda, as was seen above, seems to have been the highest-ranking official of the KISAL, the office in charge of boats. Thus, if é-nanna is the lú-má mentioned in **115** r. VII 19-20 and in **132** v. V 3-4 and ab-mud is our na-gada, then he must have been a cattle handler employed in towing the boats. Furthermore, this conclusion could establish a connection between the gu$_4$-gur-SI and the $^{d}$sùd centre supported by the considerations expressed in note 79.

<u>ur-$^{d}$gibil$_{6}$</u> is mentioned as a sipa-$^{d}$(sùd) in **120** v.II 2-4[85] and as na-gada in **29** r. V; **146** v. I 5-6.

<u>ur-kin-nir</u> is described as sipa AN in **132** r. V 11-12.

<u>ur-nin-ri$_{8}$-ru-a</u> is mentioned as sipa AN in TSŠ 723 r. III 3'-4' and as na-gada in **37** r. IV' 20'-21'; **46** r. V 10-11; **115** r. VIII 16-17; **124** r. IV 8-9 and in **125** v. II 1-2. The mention of ur-nin-ri$_{8}$-ru-a in **46** indicates that he is a middle-to high-ranking official. ur-$^{d}$nin-ri$_{8}$-ru-a should be identified with the homonymous official from Adab whose subordinate is a šùš mentioned in Š 243 (cf. *supra* p.67, note 21)

b) The IB officials[86] :

<u>AN-nu-me</u> whose complete description is IB.PA-AN / $^{d}$sùd[87] is mentioned in **93** r. II 4-5; **94** r. IV 9-10; **124** r. IV 8-9; **125** r. IV; **127** v. IV 7-8; **129** r. II 6-7; NTSŠ 262 v. II 2-3; WF 108 r. II 1-2[88] .

---

85 In the parallel passage **116** r. VIII 1-2 the characterizing element of this name has the variant KA-zi in place of sipa $^{d}$[sùd]. This latter official cannot but be identified with the na-gada gu$_{4}$-gur-SI mentioned in **210** r. I 1. This gu$_{4}$-gur-SI also belonged to the $^{d}$sùd centre.

86 The IB official, who generally belonged to the cult sphere, also appears in the documentation of Fara in connection with other officials like the abgal (cf. **37** v. II' 9'-11': a-zu$_{5}$-zu$_{5}$ nin-ul$_{4}$-gal IB abgal; **122** v. VI 2-4; WF 42 r. II 3-5: $^{d}$sùd-á-mah IB abgal), the maškim (cf. TSŠ 881 v. III 1'-3': $^{d}$sùd-da-mah-di IB maškim) and the gal-nimgir (cf. NTSŠ 262 r. II 7-8: nin-ur-sag IB gal-nimgir). It is probable that the officials who carried out this activity while they performed their function in connection with the temple, gave their services only (or also) to the administration. The IB profession has been discussed previously by I.Gelb, *Old Akkadian Insscriptions in Chicago Natural History Museum*, Fieldiana: Anthropology 44/II, Chicago 1955, p.217.

87 For the meaning of the term PA-$^{d}$sùd and its connection with PA.PA cf. *Šuruppak*, p.211.

88 The mention of AN-nu-me PA.PA in **132** v. V 13-14 is of particular interest. PA.PA is a high-ranking official whose name appears in the colophon of two anše texts **144** and **147**. The meaning of this mention cannot but be analogous to that of the mention of $^{d}$sùd in the colophons of **130**, **146** and **170**. If AN-nu-me PA.PA is, as seems likely, a variant of AN-nu-me IB PA-$^{d}$sùd, then the mentions of PA.PA and $^{d}$sùd refer to the same administrative centre. The high rank of PA.PA is also suggested by his being mentioned in the first place

AŠ-mah is mentioned with the same profession in WF 42 r.IV 2-3.

dumu-nun-šita as IB.PA-AN / $^{d}$sùd is mentioned in 10 v. V 5-6; 65 r. I 3-4; TSŠ 548 r. I' 4'-5'; WF 148 r. II 1-2. He is mentioned as IB in 47 r. II 5'-6' and 127 r. IV 4-5.

c) Middle-to high-ranking officials:

a-gestin dub-sar na-gada $^{d}$sùd in **37** v. I 1-3 is mentioned simply as dub-sar in **134** v. II 6-7; **135** r. IV 4'-5' and **146** r. III 6-7.

utu-unken-a engar $^{d}$sùd in **116** r. VII 13-14 and **120** r. II 3-4 is mentioned only as engar in **139** v. II 3-4 and **146** r. IV 2-3. 3).

In addition, nin-gu$_{10}$-nu-na-DU géme $^{d}$sùd is mentioned in a contract (cf. RTC 12 r. III 7-8) as is lú-[ ]-ta utul-AN (cf. TSŠ 881 r. IV 1'-2').

**2) The $^{d}$gibil$_6$ Centre:**

a-si$_4$ ugula $^{d}$gibil$_6$: WF 81 v. I 1-2 2).

amar-šùba na-gada $^{d}$gibil$_6$ (cf. **132** v. VI 11-13) is often mentioned with the abbreviation $^{d}$gibil$_6$ (cf. **68** r. III 7-8; **69** v. II 5-6; **89** v. I 5-II 1; **121** r. IV 4'-5'; **122** r. IV 5'-6'; **136** r. III 12-13; **142** r. II .1-2) or simply as na-gada (cf. **29** r. I 5-6; **135** v. III 4-5; TSŠ 89 r. III 4-5).

dè-dè $^{d}$gibil$_6$: **159** r. II 1-2.

é-<zi>-pa-è $^{d}$gibil$_6$: **68** r. IV 17-18; **70** r. III 2-3; **84** r. III 7'-8'; **89** v. II 2-3; **130** r. II 7-III 1; **142** r. V 3-4; **143** r. V 6-7; **170** r. II 1-2. He should be identified with the sipa-udu na-gada mentioned in **154** r.II 5-7.

é-sukkal sipa $^{d}$gibil$_6$: **29** r. VI 19-VII 1.

lugal-engar-zi $^{d}$gibil$_6$: **132** r. VI 11-12.

lugal-sèmbi $^{d}$gibil$_6$: **121** r. II 2-3; **131** r. IV 2-3; **134** r. V 1-2; **136** r. IV 7-8.

nam-mah $^{d}$nin-(ki) $^{d}$gibil$_6$[89] : **116** r. II 13-15; **124** r. VIII 14-16; **159** r. I 2-4. This official could perhaps be identified with the homonymous engar-sipa mentioned in TSŠ 522 r. III 9.

ur-dumu-zi sipa $^{d}$gibil$_6$: **121** v. V 1-2 and only as $^{d}$gibil$_6$ in **116** v. I 1-2.

---

in a sequence of officials both in **143** r. I 1 and in **175** r. I 2. This list includes the sanga-GAR, the sa$_{12}$-du$_5$, the šùš, the enku, the gal-nimgir and the <gal>-sukkal.

89 The mention of an anonymous official $^{d}$nin $^{d}$gibil$_6$, the beneficiary of 3 gur of barley in **29** r. VI 2-3, could imply the name nam-mah.

**3) The kin-nir Centre:**

kur-ra-á-gal na-gada kin-nir: **115** r. III 13-15; **121** r. VI 4-6; **122** r. V 1'-3'; and only as kin-nir in **86** r. I 1-3 and **124** r. VII 13-14; and only as na-gada in **123** r. IV 3'-4' and **128** r. V 9-10.

nì-šà-ta-nu-è engar kin-nir: **115** r. VII 4-7; **121** v. I 10'-12'; **122** r. VIII 3'-4'.

amar-kù kin-nir: **98** r. II 18'-19'; **127** r. III 5-6; **128** r. II 10-11; **132** v. VII 15-16; **134** r. IV 12-13. This official should probably be identified with the engar-sipa mentioned in TSŠ 522 r. III 4.

amar-šùba kin-nir: **121** r. VI 11'-12'; **124** r. III 7-8; **125** r. II 7-8; **126** r. II 1-2.

é-du$_{10}$ kin-nir: **14** r. V 7-8.26) KA-ni gudu$_4$ kin-nir: **116** r. I 16-17; **117** v. II 2'-4'.

lugal-du$_{10}$ kin-nir: **127** v. IV 1-2; **128** v. III 1-2; **134** v. V 3-4.

úr-NI $^{d}$kin-nir: **136** v. V 1-2.

This latter official should probably be identified with the beneficiary/consignee of the sheep mentioned in WF 126 v. I 1; CT 50, 20 r. I 2' and especially with the homonymous úr-NI šubur ú-dul$_4$ mentioned in **115** r. II 12-14[90] . Now šubur ú-dul$_4$ is the official mentioned in the colophon of **137** and perhaps in **121**. The meaning of the mention in the colophons of these texts should be regarded as analogous to that of $^{d}$sùd and PA.PA discussed above. The proposed identification suggests a relationship between the activity of šubur ú-dul$_4$ and the centre kin-nir; and it is likely that this official was the person (or one of the persons) in charge of the centre in question[91] .

---

90 The so-called archive of úr-NI identified in the texts at Pennsylvania University (cf. S.N.Kramer, *New Tablets from Fara*, JAOS 55 [1953], pp.110-131) has not so far been published. The tablets could have formed part of the archives of this centre and in particular of the šubur ú-dul$_4$.

91 According to this hypothesis several other officials could have belonged to the kin-nir centre: AN-nu-me šubur ú-dul$_4$ (**115** r. III 8-10; **117** r. IV 3-5); KA-ni-zi šubur/ú-dul$_4$ (**14** r. X 2-3; **54** r. II 1-2; TSŠ 47 v. II 3'-4'); lu-lu šubur (**121** r. VI 10-11; **122** r. V 7'-8'; **127** r. II 3-4; **134** r. VI 11-12); á-ág-du$_{10}$ ú-dul$_4$ (**121** v. I 12'-13'; **123** v. II 5; **133** r. III 11'-12'); bil$_x$-á-nu-kúš ú-dul$_4$ (**11** v. VI 15-VII 1). We have no elements to support this, but it cannot be excluded that the last-mentioned official could be identified with the homonymous gú-iš-

But the centres $^{d}$sùd, $^{d}$gibil$_{6}$ and kin-nir which from the documentation seem to be the most important are not the only temple centres or centres with the name of a divinity connected with animal breeding which could be identified. Two texts, until now considered votive offerings, indicate the existence of other centres. These texts are CT 50, 23 and WF 126.

**CT 50, 23**

| | | | | |
|---|---|---|---|---|
| r. | I | 1) | 1 gu$_{4}$-niga | 1 fattened ox |
| | | 2) | 6 gu$_{4}$-ú | 6 oxen fed with grass |
| | | 3) | $^{d}$sùd | (from the centre of) Sud |
| | | 4) | 3 gu$_{4}$-niga | 3 fattened oxen |
| | | 5) | 6 gu$_{4}$-ú | 6 oxen fed with grass |
| | | 6) | $^{d}$gibil$_{6}$ | (from the centre of) Gibil |
| | II | 1) | 3 $^{d}$en-líl$^{ki}$ | 3 ( oxen from the centre of) Enlil/Nippur |
| | | 2) | 2 gu$_{4}$ | 2 oxen |
| | | 3) | 6 gu$_{4}$-ú | 6 oxen fed with grass |
| | | 4) | kin-nir | (from the centre of) Kinnir |
| | | 5) | 7 gu$_{4}$ | 7 oxen |
| | | 6) | EN.ZU$^{ki}$ | (from the centre of) Su'en |
| v. | I | 1) | 7 gu$_{4}$ | 7 oxen |
| | | 2) | utu$^{ki}$ | (from the centre of) Utu |
| | | 3) | 1 gu$_{4}$-numun-niga | 1 fattened ox for the seader-plow[92] |

---

DU mentioned in TSŠ 878 v.I 2-3. gú-iš-DU$^{ki}$ is a toponym mentioned several times in **37** r. II' 2'; III' 5'; 11'.

92 This sort of ox, gu$_{4}$-numun, is mentioned in Neosumerian documentation from Lagaš (cf. DAS, 282 r.1 et passim; SAT 1, 234 r.1; 236 r.1 et passim; 397 r.1; SNATBM, 321 r. 1-4 and also MVN 17, 14 r.1: 3 gu$_{4}$-numun-giš. These last oxen, gu$_{4}$-numun-giš, are

| | | | |
|---|---|---|---|
| | 4) | dumu-<nun>-šita | (by) Dumununšita |
| II | 1) | an-šè-gú 42 gu$_4$ | A total of 42 oxen |
| | 2) | su-si | the tanner/skinner[93] |
| | 3) | šu-ba$_4$-ti | has received |

The text is a register of contributions made by the Sud, Gibil, Enlil, Kinnir, Suen and Utu centres and by dumu-<nun>-šita mentioned in v. I 3-4. This latter should be identified with the dumu-nun-šita IB employed in the Sud centre (cf. *supra*, p.122, b)[94] . The su-si official is who received the animals. In addition to the already known centres $^{d}$sùd, $^{d}$gibil$_6$ and kin-nir, the names of others are mentioned: $^{d}$en-líl$^{ki}$, $^{d}$EN.ZU$^{ki}$ and utu$^{ki}$. While the first and last are mentioned elsewhere in the documentation of Fara, the second, $^{d}$EN.ZU$^{ki}$, is never mentioned.

**WF 126**

| | | | | |
|---|---|---|---|---|
| r. | I | 1) | 2 udu-nita | 2 rams |
| | | 2) | énsi-GAR | (from the) Ensi-GAR |
| | | 3) | su-su-ma | (for) Susuma |
| | | 4) | 1 (u) 1 (m) énsi-GAR* | 1 (ram and) 1 (goat from the) Ensi-GAR |
| | | 5) | 1 (m) $^{d}$sùd | 1 (goat from the centre) Sud |
| | | 6) | amar-abzu | for Amarabzu |
| | | 7) | 1 (m) kin-nir | 1 (goat from the centre) Kinnir |
| | II | 1) | en-kalam-du$_{10}$ | (for) Enkalamdu |
| | | 2) | 1 (m) $^{d}$sùd | 1 (goat from the centre) Sud |
| | | 3) | 1 (m) $^{d}$dumu-zi 1 (goat from the centre) Dumuzi | |
| | | 4) | 1 (m) kin-nir | 1 (goat from the centre) Kinnir |

summarized in the šu-nígin with the other gu$_4$-numun recorded in the tablet) and from Nippur (cf. TMH I-II, 303 r.1; NATN, 609 r.1; 646 r.1; 701 r.1).

93 For the interpretation of su-si (akk. suššikku) as "Abdecker" cf. D.O.Edzard, ZA 66, p.164.

94 Dumununšita recur also in **52** r. II 1, a text of assignement of barley as food for oxen and donkeys, and for seeding.

| | | | |
|---|---|---|---|
| | 5) | 1 (u) 1 (m) é-géme | 1 (ram) and 1 (goat from the) é-géme |
| | 6) | 1 (m) $^{d}$nin-URUDU | 1 (goat from the centre of) Nin.URUDU |
| | 7) | é-al$_{6}$-la | for the Ealla |
| III | 1) | 2 (m) énsi-GAR | 2 (goats from the) Ensi-GAR |
| | 2) | kun-gá | for Kunga |
| | 3) | 1(u) 2 (m) énsi-GAR | 1 (ram) 2 (goats from the) Ensi-GAR |
| | 4) | ur-$^{d}$gú-lá | for Urgula |
| | 5) | 1 (m) GÁNA.KÚ | 1 (goat from) PN$^{?}$ |
| | 6) | 1 (m) šubur | 1 (goat from) Šubur (the subordinate of) |
| | 7) | abzu-ki-du$_{10}$ Abzukidu | |
| | 8) | $^{d}$gibil$_{6}$ | (for the centre of) Gibil |
| v. I | 1) | 1 (m) úr-[m]ud 1 (goat from) Urmud | |
| | 2) | 1 (m) amar-abzu | 1 (goat from) Amarabzu |
| | 3) | 2 (u) 2 (m) dumu-ambar | 2 (rams) and 2(goats from)Dumuambar |
| | 4) | lu-lu | (the subordinate of) Lulu |
| | 5) | GA[R].GU.NUN | for the Gununsur |
| | 6) | 3 (u) lugal-UŠ | 3 (rams from) Lugalus |
| | 7) | 1 (u) lugal-ki-dúr-du$_{10}$ | 1 (ram from) Lugalkidurdu |
| | 8) | *d[u]-du* | (the subordinate of) Dudu. |
| II | 1) | 3 (u) 3 (m) lugal-ki-dúr-du$_{10}$ | 3 (rams) and 3 (goats from) Lugalkidurdu |
| | 2) | sagi | the sagi (or the subordinate of the gal-sagi) |
| | 3) | 1 (u) 1 (m) me-an-si | 1 (ram) 1 (goat from) Meansi |
| | 4) | lam-ma | (subordinate of) Lamma/for Lamma |
| | 5) | [p]a$_{4}$-nu-šè | for Panuše/the subordinate of Panuše |
| | 6) | 1 (m) $^{d}$en-líl$^{ki}$ | 1 (goat from the centre) Enlil |
| | 7) | blank | |
| III | 1) | an-šè-gú | For a total of |
| | 2) | 15 udu | 15 rams |
| | 3) | 23 LAK 20 | 23 goats |

4) udu-kú for eating.

5) blank

(m = LAK 20; u = udu)

The structure of this text is not frequent in the documentation of Fara. It is made up of 10 sections each of which is divided into two parts. The first part consists of one or two items, professional names and personal names generally followed by a characterizing element or the names of administrative centres. These items are preceded by the indication of the type and of the quantity of goods in question, rams (udu) and/or goats (megida)[95] . The second part has just one item, an anthroponym without any indication of a characterizing element (Susuma, Amarabzu, Enkalamdu, Kunga, Urgula and Panuše), the name of an administrative centre (Ealla, Gibil) or a professional name (GAR.GU.NUN.<SUR>) which is not preceded by any indication of goods. The only exception to this is the tenth section. This has only one part (1 $^{d}$en-líl$^{ki}$). After the summary of the animals listed in the text, the colophon contains the clause udu-kú,"sheep for eating". But if the reasons for the transactions recorded are clear, neither the beneficiary nor the consignee of the goods appears equally clearly.

From the comparison with the preceding text, we have preferred to consider the anthroponyms or the professional names or the centres preceded by an indication of the type of goods as the consignees, that is, those who are listed in the first part of each section, and the anthroponym or the centre or the professional name which followed as the beneficiary. But it cannot be excluded that the first part of each section could indicate the beneficiaries and the second part the consignees of the good on the analogy of **104** and its parallel **105**, one of the very rare texts toghether with **105** which is similar in structure to WF 126.

However we interpret WF 126, it mentions, just like CT 50, 23, a series of centres identified by a divine name. In addition to the $^{d}$sùd, $^{d}$gibil$_{6}$ and kin-nir centres, the following centres are mentioned: $^{d}$en-lil$^{ki}$ in both texts, utu$^{ki}$[96] in CT 50, 23 and

---

[95] For the interpretation of LAK 20 as a term for "male goat" cf. TLAT, p.85, 4.

[96] There is one mention of this centre as a toponym of the provenance of an uru-DU (cf. **13** v. I 1-4).

$^{d}$dumu-zi[97] and $^{d}$nin-URUDU[98] in WF 126. It is interesting to observe that in this latter text these centres are mentioned both as beneficiaries and as consignees in relation to the other administrative centres of Šuruppak like the é-géme, the é-al-la and the offices of the énsi and the GAR.GU.NUN.SUR. In our opinion, this connection means that these centres were an integral part of the administration of Fara and of equal rank with the main organizations of the state even though they were probably temple organizations.

The existence of centres identified by a divine name and connected with cattle breeding seems to be fairly clear on the basis of the evidence thus far presented. Less clear, however, is their location. Some of these centres, like $^{d}$sùd, $^{d}$gibil$_{6}$ and kin-nir, must have been in Šuruppak or in its immediate surroundings not only because both the goddess Sud and the god Gibil were tutelary divinities of the city but especially because of the large number of personnel who belonged to these centres and who are mentioned in texts of almost all types, in particular in those concerning barley, anše and allotment fields.

The location of the $^{d}$en-lil$^{ki}$, utu$^{ki}$, $^{d}$EN.ZU, $^{d}$dumu-zi and $^{d}$nin-URUDU centres appears to be more problematic. Since the toponym $^{d}$en-lil$^{ki}$ indicated at that time, and in subsequent periods, the city of Nippur, it seems difficult that it should indicate anywhere else in spite of the fact that it was included in a list of centres linked together by a divine name. In our opinion, it is a cattle breeding centre under the jurisdiction of the temple administration of Enlil in Nippur. The centre utu$^{ki}$ is mentioned as a toponym from which abzu-ki-du$_{10}$ came; he was an uru-DU and a subordinate of the nimgir ur-dumu-nun (cf. **13** v. I 4). Now we know that all the uru-DU are "foreign" personnel who come both from the most important Sumerian cites like Adab, Lagaš, Nippur, Umma and Uruk and from minor cities like ši-lum (probably a variant of šul-lum$^{ki}$), tu$^{ki}$, ùru-za-gu and the above-mentioned utu$^{ki}$. For reasons of internal coherence we must suppose that these minor cities were located outside Šuruppak. If two of the five centres are located outside Šuruppak then it is

97 ba-za ì-du$_{8}$ $^{d}$dumu-zi is in the employ of the $^{d}$dumu-zi centre (cf. *supra*, p.118, note 81). It is probable that this centre should be identified with the é-dumu-zi mentioned in **13** v. IV 1-2 where a certain sikil is employed.

98 The centre $^{d}$nin-URUDU is not mentioned elsewhere in the documentation of Fara.

probable that this should also be true for the remaining three[99]. If this deduction is correct we must posit an economic and administrative organization with a communitarian character involving various Sumerian cities, as least as far as cattle breeding was concerned[100]. Since the personnel who belonged to these communitarian cattle breeding centres, like the uru-DU personnel of the é-gal-nimgir, was the responsibility of the central administration of Šuruppak, we must conclude that this organization which linked various Sumerian cities had its epicentre in that same city.

---

99 It is possible that a location outside Šuruppak could be posited for the é-lugal. In fact, this centre is mentioned in the documentation of Fara exclusively in relation to officials connected with cattle breeding or with the cult. But it is not clear from the documentation what exactly the role of the lugal was in Sumerian society at the time of the archives of Fara, but it seems difficult to accept for that period the model proposed by Th.Jacobsen, ZA 57, p.122 which sees the lugal and the en juxtaposed in the roles of military and religious leaders. In fact, it seems surprising from the documents of Fara that the role of the lugal should be linked with the cult rather than with the political and military spheres.

100 This seems to be further confirmed by the mention of the sipa-$^{d}$sud, ur-$^{d}$nin-ri$_{8}$-ru-a, from Adab and of the šùš, en-šà-ge, from Kullab (cf. *supra*, p.67, note 21).

## 3) THE CRAFTWORKERS' CORPORATIONS

In the barley texts of the II group the following professional names are mentioned, in addition to the lú-má who were employed in the KISAL: the énsi-GAR and the lú-má-gal-gal, the šu-$ku_6$ who were subordinates of the enku and the é-géme and the personnel who belonged to the breeding centres: ašgab, $azlag_4$, GU.ŠU.$DU_8$, lú-$^{giš}$BÙLUG, lú-tir, lùmgi, $munu_4$-mú, muš-$lah_4$, mušen-dù, nagar, simug, šitim, šùš, túg-$du_8$, ùsan-dù, utul, and zadim[101] : these represent many categories of workers and artisans. Besides these artisans, there were other workers employed in the gardens and orchards: the nu-$kiri_6$, the kínda and the ú-a. In texts of other types there were different $bahar_4$, galla$^{lá}$ and kurušda. For many of these professions ugulas are mentioned (kìnda, nagar, simug, túg-$du_8$, zadim) as are corporation heads (gal-ašgab, gal-$azlag_4$, gal-$bahar_4$, gal-galla$^{lá}$, gal-$kiri_6$, gal-kínda, gal-nagar, gal-simug, gal-šitim and gal-zadim).

One could, therefore, conclude that within each category of craftworkers there was a well defined hierarchy as for the other professions and that the greater part of these craftworkers belonged to the administration of the é-uru centre[102] . At the head of each corporation there must have been a gal-Prof.N, at an intermediate level the ugulas, generally two or three per category, whose task was the supervision of the specialized workers. In the surviving documentation, however, there is not

---

[101] The professions which recur most frequently in the barley texts of II group are: nagar (16 times), simug (12 times), lú-$^{giš}$BÙLUG (7 times) and šitim (6 times).

[102] Some artisans also work in the é-gal in the context of their respective im-ru. These are: ad-KID, $bahar_4$, dilmun, kínda, $munu_4$, túg-$du_8$ and zadim with their respective ugulas. Now, with the exception of ad-KID, dilmun and $munu_4$ who worked only in the sphere of the é-gal, the artisans of all the other categories, at least on the basis of our documentation, were employed in the two administrative centres. But we do not know what the relationship was between these artisans and their respective corporations which seem to have belonged to the administrative centre of the uru. In other words, it escapes us whether these artisans, wherever they worked, were always subordinates of the corporation heads. This is also the case of those artisans who within the same administrative centre worked in different offices than the gal-Prof.N. This was the case of the nagar, simug and the ašgab who worked in the KISAL and of the ùsan-dù of the office of the enku.

always a mention of ugulas or the gal-Prof.N for all the categories in question. In the documentation there is no mention of apprentices who certainly must have existed perhaps because their payment was recorded in registers different from those which have survived.

4) THE OFFICE OF THE ENKU

In the analysis of the guruš texts we identified a group of officials who provided contingents for conscription and who belonged to the same office. These were: nimgir-teme-na, $^{d}$sùd-anzu, šà-ezen, ur-$^{d}$nin-mú and šubur (**191** r. III 3'-6'; **194** r. I 1-II 2). While the last-mentioned is followed by a characterizing element ùsan-dù (cf. also for the mention of this official CT 50, 5 r. II 1-2), the first four are mentioned in sequence in TSŠ 969, a SI.NUxŠUŠ text, and have no characterizing element. **194** lists, in its surviving lines, three of these officials and concludes in r. II 3 with the mention of the professional name enku. This mention could refer both to the last-mentioned official in the list, šubur ùsan-dù, or to all the officials listed. Now we can observe that **a**) one of the sections of **46** (r. IV 3-8) lists two officials (KA-ṭar$^{?}$-zi ùsan-dù nimgir-teme-na šu-ku$_6$ enku) and concludes with the mention of the enku, **b**) one of the officials (nimgir-teme-na) in this section coincides with one of the anthroponyms of our group and **c**) the only official in the section of **46** which precedes that already mentioned (r. IV 1-2) is the šu-ku$_6$ ur-$^{d}$nin-mú, which coincides with one of the anthroponyms of our group. We must conclude that the professional name enku in both texts refers to all the officials mentioned and that nimgir-teme-na and ur-$^{d}$nin-mú are two šu-ku$_6$ employed in the office of enku. With regard to the remaining two, $^{d}$sùd-anzu and šà-ezen, we do not know their profession. šà-ezen is mentioned exclusively in the already-mentioned texts **191**, **192** and TSŠ 969 while $^{d}$sùd-anzu is one of the most common anthroponyms in the documentation of Fara. However, the mention in sequence with other already identified officials renders it likely that they were also šu-ku$_6$ or ùsan-dù .

But these officials are not the only ones in the employ of the enku. At least six others, together with their subordinates, belong to this office. They are:

a-nun-pà who is mentioned as being in the employ of the enku in **121** r. VI 7-8; **122** r. V 4'-5'; **127** v. II 6-7; **132** r. VI 5-6; **153** r. II 3-4 even though it is impossible to deduce his profession from the documentation. It is probable that some of the anthroponyms related to the same official belong to the same office; this is the case of šà-gù-ba a-nun-pà mentioned in **115** r. IX 5-6 and **171** r. III 5'-6' and a-nun-$^{d}$sùd-da a-nun-<pà> in **115** v. III 4-5.

amar-$^{d}$IB šu-ku$_6$ enku who is the superior of har-tu-$^{d}$sùd (**23** v. IV 11-14 and parallels). We do not know the profession of har-tu-$^{d}$sùd but from a comparison with the following passages: har-tu-$^{d}$sùd ur-$^{d}$nin-<mù> (**72** r. I 5-6; **73** v. I 8-9; **124** v. V 10-11); har-tu-$^{d}$sùd šà-gú-ba (**87** r. I 4-5); šà-gú-ba ur-$^{d}$nin-<mú> (**68** r. VI 13-14 and parallel texts; **121** r. II 4'-5'; **147** r. II 1-2); šà-gú-ba šu-ku$_6$ (**74** v. IV 6-7; **121** r. V 10-11; **122** r. IV 11-12; **142** r. III 5-6) and ur-$^{d}$nin-mú šu-ku$_6$ (**46** r. IV 1-2) we can suppose that har-tu-$^{d}$sùd, the subordinate of amar-$^{d}$IB, should be identified with the homonymous official who was related to the šu-ku$_6$ šà-gú-ba and ur-$^{d}$nin-mù and was employed in fishing.

KA-ni é-enku is mentioned in **35** r. V 7-8. This KA-ni could be an abbreviation for KA-ni-zi on the basis of a comparison of the following passages: KA-ni-zi ùsan-dù (**121** v. II 3'-4'; **122** v. I 2-3; **132** r. VI 13-14); KA-ni-zi šubur (**14** r. X 2-3) and šubur ùsan-dù enku (**194** r. II 1-3). The probable presence of different ùsan-dù could lead us to hypothesize that $^{d}$sùd-anzu, one of the officials mentioned together with šubur in **194** r. I 4, should be identified with the homonymous ùsan-dù in **23** v. II 2-3 and **28** r. III 1-2[103] .

lam-ma enku is mentioned in **47** r. I 4-5 and **195** v. I 1-2. The documentation does not provide us with elements to identify this anthroponym with any of the homonyms mentioned there.

uš-dù enku. This anthroponym is mentioned in **195** r. VI 3-4.

AK-utu maškim enku is mentioned in **14** r. X 17-19. The official must be the same as the maškim who is the subordinate of the ugula-maškim é-ki-ba mentioned in **19** v. II 2-3[104] .

---

[103] If KA-ni é-enku is to be identified with KA-ni-zi ùsan-dù, then the question must be raised whether KA-tar-zi, the ùsan-dù <enku> mentioned in **46** r. IV 3-4 but not elsewhere attested with this characterizing element, should be identified with KA-ni-zi.

[104] Of course, this is not the only maškim mentioned as being the subordinate of a high-ranking official. In fact a-da (**115** v. I 10-12) and AN-nu-me (**14** v. V 7-9) are maškim of the sa$_{12}$-du$_5$; AN-nu-me is maškim of the šùš (**68** v. I 11-13; **134** r. V 10-12); AK is maškim of the sanga-GAR (TSŠ 627 r.II 7-III 3). In addition, unnamed maškim are

In conclusion, a considerable number of officials of various levels belonged to the office of the enku; but the workers connected with that office must have been much more numerous in agreement with the mention of the 60 guruš which the enku provides for conscription (cf. **188** r. V 5 but also **192** v. I 1; **193** r. IV 6 and **195** v. I 1) The function of the numerous šu-$ku_6$ and the ùsan-dù among the officials who belonged to the enku is not clear. In fact, the role of the enku within the administration must have been that of a "collector of tributes", if the Akkadian equivalent ***mākisu*** in the Proto-lu lexical lists of the Old Babylonian period is also valid for this one. It should be noted that in this period there was an official in Fara, the dam-$kas_4$, interpreted by us as a *tapras* form of ***makāsu*** (cf. G.Visicato, *Some Aspects of the Administrative Organization of Fara*, Or 61 (1992), p.97 note 8), who must have been in charge of this activity. If we admit that the enku at the period of our archives had the same functions as that of later periods, then the enku and the dam-$kas_4$ were the same official, that is, dam-$kas_4$ was the Semitic term for enku. Alternatively the dam-$kas_4$ and the enku were different officials and the latter must have had another function different from that of later periods.

---

mentioned who are subordinates of the énsi-GAR-gal (WF 144 r. II 1-2); of the lugal (CT 50, 15 r. II 2-3) and of da-da sanga-GAR of Nippur (TSŠ 627 r. I 2-4). It should, however, be observed that unlike the maškim of the enku, these maškim do not appear among those mentioned in the barley texts of the I group who were subordinate to two ugula maškims of the é-gal, namely, é-ki-ba and har-tu-$^{d}$sùd.

# CONCLUSION

In our study of the texts of Fara two aspects in particular have been stressed; in the first place, the structure of the administrative system of Fara and, in the second place, the relationships which existed among a group of Sumerian cities between the end of ED II and the beginning of ED III. These two aspects have important implications both for the knowledge of that particular historical period, until now rather obscure, and what must have been the structure of Sumerian society during the second half of the III millenium. To these two aspects and to their implications, we would like to devote our concluding remarks.

**A)** In the previous chapter we have established and analysed a series of relationships which connected the various offices mentioned in the documentation with the administrative centres of the é-gal and the é-uru and we have sketched the function of these offices, where this has been possible and only in rough outline because of the lack of data. In addition, we have ascertained the relationship between these offices and the intermediate structures which were their backbone and for which the ugulas, nimgirs, dam-gàrs etc, were responsible. In Table 2 we have proposed an organizational chart of how the whole administration of Fara might have been structured.

This organizational chart gathers together what we have been able to deduce from the documentation. From this, the role of the é-géme stands out as the operative office of the énsi and of the whole administration of Šuruppak. This was where ultimate responsibility lay for the entire production of grain and its derivates and for cattle breeding. The whole operation was coordinated through some dub-sars, engars and ugulas who were their subordinates. The proposed organizational chart is an investigative tool which schematically enables us to relate the greater part of the data derived from the analysis of the texts, even though all the problems proposed by the documentation cannot solved nor all the elements which are available to us fitted into the picture. For example, we know that most of the lú-má are subordinates of the nu-bànda in charge of the office of the KISAL but that other lú-má are subordinates both of the ugula énsi-GAR and of the lú-má-gal-gal; but we know nothing of the relationship which must have existed between these offices.

**Table 1**

**The Organization Chart of the E D Šuruppak Administration**

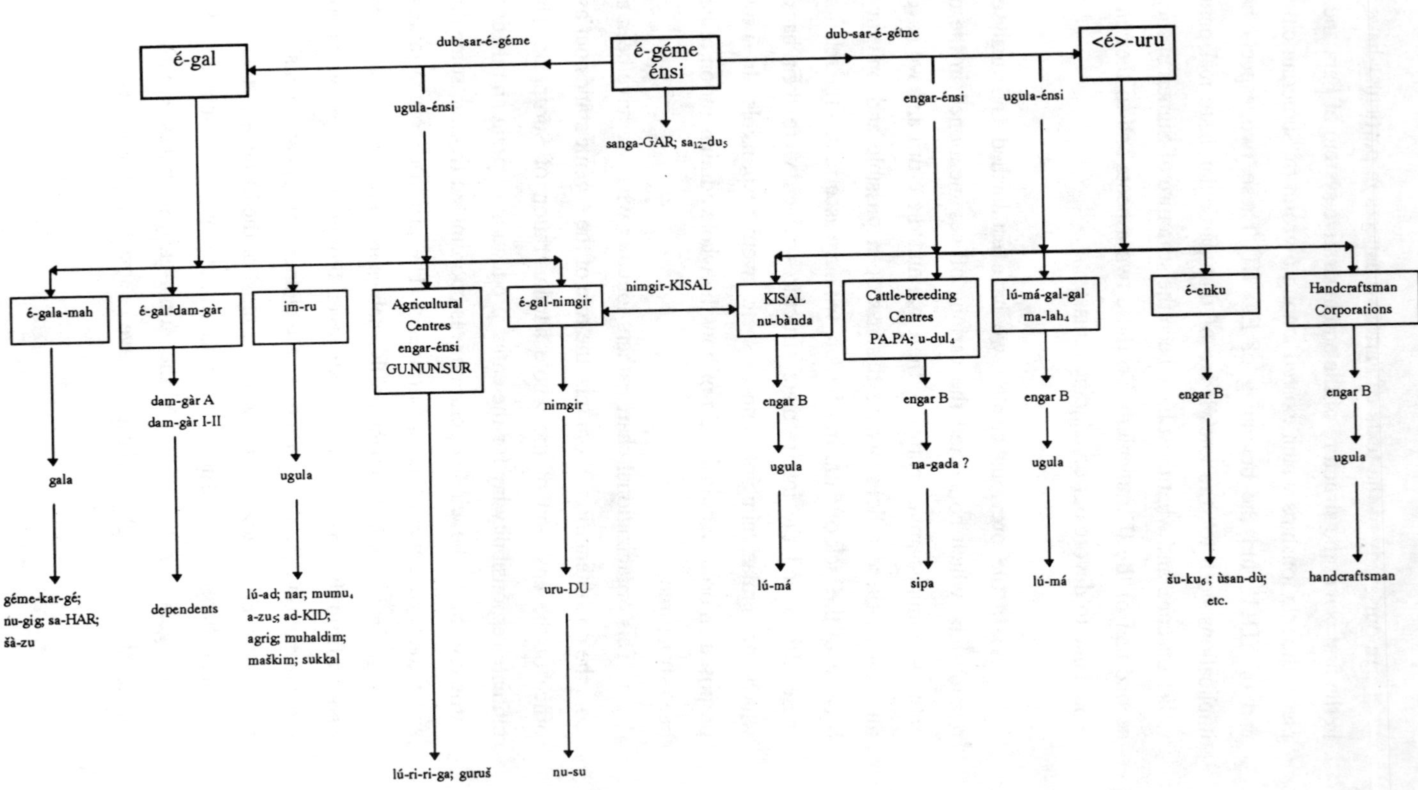

In fact, all the lú-má are listed together in a single document, the dub-lú-má **23**. Again, the relationship between the engar-énsi and the Class A and B engars is unknown even though we have succeeded in identifying, with a certain degree of probability, the function of each category of official. The engar-énsis, who are probably the same as the engars of the é-géme, were in charge of the seed barley for the aša$_5$-šuku and probably also of the barley for rations and of the management of the state lands (cf. *Šuruppak*, pp.92; 101; 220-221); they receive considerable quantities of barley in the texts of the I group and also quantities of oil in CT 50, 14. The Class A engars were responsible for the barley allocated to the subordinates listed in entire sections of the texts of the II group but they are not themselves mentioned as beneficiaries of allocations. The Class B engars, on the other hand, were responsible for the barley allocated to single beneficiaries mentioned in the texts of the II group within the sections for which the Class A engars were responsible; they are also mentioned in these latter texts as beneficiaries of allocations of barley. These Class B engars, unlike those of Class A, seem to have been connected with particular offices or professional corporations (cf. *ibidem*, p.100). Since a relationship of subordination is never explicitly indicated among these categories of engars, we must regard their relationship not as directly hierarchical but as consisting of a different level of responsibility in the management of the barley.

The office of the gal-nimgir which was, one the one hand, connected to the administrative centre of the é-gal, appears as an organizational system of a regional type whose workers come from various Sumerian cities. On the other hand, it appears to be linked with the second centre, the uru. In fact, a nimgir with some "foreign" lú-má works in the office of the KISAL and it is possible that other nimgirs worked in the offices of the má-lah$_4$, the gal-galla and é-al-la. In many cases, however, the reason for these connections escapes us even if we can guess that all were, in the last analysis, connected with communications.

We know almost nothing about the activity of the agricultural centres of the state apart from the fact they gave employment both to the vast majority of the guruš recruited for war and to the lú-ri-ri-ga mentioned in **1**. We know that these centres must have been under the responsibility of the engar-énsis who were in charge of the distribution of barley and probably also of the GU.NUN.SUR. In a similar way, in spite of the detailed analysis made in chapter III, the little we know about the cattle breeding centres is confined to the personnel who belonged to them and to the officials who were in charge.

Finally, if the particular characteristics of the documentation have, on the one hand, enabled us to identify a series of organizational structures, on the other, they have given us few elements to establish certain and clear relationships between the various sectors of the administration. In particular, they have given us no information on how those centres involved in the production of goods actually worked.

**B)** The relationship between Šuruppak and the other cities of Babylonia has already been amply discussed (cf. *Šuruppak*, pp.10-21). To what has already been said we would like to add the following observations:

1) There is the mention of over 2,000 subordinates belonging to the im-rus of the é-gal; among these were 350 lú-ad, 210 agrig, 140 maškim, 140 sukkal, 140 muhaldim, 70 a-zu$_5$ and 70 nar. There were about 80 gala officials who belonged to the office of the gala-mah of the é-gal. There were the 300 lú-má mentioned in 187 as being in the employ of the KISAL and of the énsi-GAR[105].
2) There are mentioned several officials from other cities:
   a) a maškim-gi$_4$ of Nippur, har-tu-$^d$sùd, a homonym of the ugula-maškim in charge of one of the im-rus of the é-gal (cf. *supra*, p.23) and of various maškim from Adab, Kès, IM, Uruk and Nippur;
   b) several gala from Uruk and Šullum;
   c) several lú-má from Adab, Nippur, Umma, Uruk and from other minor cities like a-hu-ti$^{ki}$, gú-iš-DU$^{ki}$ and URUxA;
   d) several artisans (lú-$^{giš}$BÙLUG, munu$_4$-mú, šùš and zadim) and nar from Adab, Šullum, Kullab, Kèš, Umma and Uruk and a dub-sar-mah from IL (cf. TSŠ 430 r. II' 1'-2').
3) The existence of an office, that of the gal-nimgir, to which about seventy uru-DU, all "foreigners" belong.
4) The real possibility that several cattle breeding centres were located outside the city perimeter of Šuruppak.

---

105 It should be noted that with regard to the 300 enlisted lú-má of **187**, the already-mentioned dub-lú-má records only 73 workers who receive allocations of barley (cf. *Šuruppa*k, p.130).

5) The fact that all the subordinates, wherever they came from, were maintained by the administration of Šuruppak.

The above suggests that there were important wide-ranging relations not only of a military nature but also, economic, administrative and political between Šuruppak and other sumerian cities and the activity of a fairly large number of the subordinates of the organizational system of Šuruppak could not have been limited exclusively to the city area.

In fact, the number of people employed in non-productive activities of point 1) seems to have been very high for the needs and the possibilities of a city state of about 30,000 inhabitants.

This consideration is of particular importance given the large number of scribes. In the administrative documentation of Fara about 90 individuals are mentioned who have the professional name dub-sar as a characterizing element. Since the documentation refers to the last years of Fara (cf. *Šuruppak*, p.8-9), these officials must have been employed by the administration contemporaneously. Now, to evaluate the relevance of the activity of this number of dub-sars we must make the following observations[106] :

a) In the almost 1,600 administrative documents from ED IIIb Girsu which refer to the reigns of Enentarzi, Lugalanda and Uruinimgina about fifty dub-sars and four dub-sar-mah are mentioned. Of these dub-sars, eight are mentioned exclusively in the texts from the reign of Enentarzi, five exclusively in texts from the reign of Lugalanda and nine exclusively in the reign of Uru'inimgina; while six are mentioned in texts from both the reigns of Enentarzi and Lugalanda, nine in texts from the time of Lugalanda and Uru'inimgina and only five in texts dating from the reigns of all three kings. This means that even if the dub-sars mentioned in the whole documentation are more than fifty, in fact, not more than thirty must have been active at the same time.
b) In the administrative documentation of Zabalam relative to the years when Lugalzagesi was énsi of Umma and which comprises about a hundred tablets

---

106 These observations are the preliminary results of a study by the author, *The Mesopotamian Scribes in Administrative Documentation from the Earliest Times to the Sargonic Period*, (forthcoming).

of various types (cf. M.A.Powell, *Texts from the Time of Lugalzagesi*, HUCA 49 (1978), pp.1-58) about ten dub-sars are mentioned.

c) In the administrative documentation with about 3,000 published tablets relative to the whole Sargonic period and coming from different sites[107], a total of about 150 dub-sars are mentioned. As can be seen from the Table 3, they can be divided according to site of provenance and period.

## Table 3

| Site | Num. dub-sar | Num. Texts | Period |
|---|---|---|---|
| **Adab** | 22<br>1 dub-sar-mah | about 300[108] | Šark. |
| **Ešnunna** | 6 | 223 | Clas. Sarg. |
| **Gasur** | 5 | 222 | Clas. Sarg. |
| **Girsu** | 56<br>1 dub-sar-mah | about 1800 | Clas. Sarg. |
| **Himrin** | 4 | 50 | Clas. Sarg. |
| **Kiš** | 5 | 68 | Clas. Sarg. |
| **Me-ság archive** | 6<br>2 dub-sar-mah | about 160[109] | Clas. Sarg. |
| **Nippur** | 24 | about 400 | 5 Early Sarg.<br>5 Naram[110].<br>14 Šark. |

---

[107] For the provenance, place of publication, dating and the present state of knowledge of the documentation of the whole Sargonic period cf. B.R.Foster, *Archive and Record-Keeping in Sargonic Mesopotamia*, ZA 72 (1982), pp.4-7.

[108] These 300 texts published in OIP 14 and in Y.Zhi, *Sargonic Inscriptions from Adab*, Changchun 1988, p.285-349, are coming from Chicago University collections. There are, also, 600 unpublished texts in Istanbul Museum (Y.Zhi, op, cit., p.3).

[109] Of these texts, 96 are been published by G.Hackman in BIN 8, 13 in TLAT, nos.33-45. The remaining texts are will be published by S.Bridges, *The Mesag Estate: A Study of Sargonic Society and Economy*, (unpublished dissertation).

| Susa | 4 | 91 | Clas. Sarg. |
|---|---|---|---|
| Umma | 38<br>1 dub-sar-gal<br>2 dub-sar-mah | 506[111] | 16 Early Sarg.<br>22 Clas. Sarg |
| Ur | 3 | 50 | Early-Clas. Sarg. |

Šark = Šar-kali-šarri; Naram. = Naram-Sin;
Clas.Sarg.=Classical Sargonic (Naram-Sin-Šar-kali-šarri);
Early Sarg.= Early Sargonic (Sargon-Maništušu).

While taking into account that part of the documentation is still to be published, it seems probable, from the data contained in this table, that no more than one hundred scribes carried out their activity contemporaneously throughout the empire.

d) Only in the very extensive documentation relating to the period of the III dynasty of Ur does the number of dub-sar mentioned seem to amount to 1,600[112]. It seems, however, that the characterizing element dub-sar which accompanies the personal name indicates only that he had been awarded an academic title by the é-dub-ba, that is, the scribal school, without this implying that he in fact exercised the profession of scribe[113]. On the basis of this observation and keeping in mind that the entire neo-Sumerian documentation covers at least four generations, we can reasonably suppose that only a few

110 The number of active scribes in Nippur during the reign of Naramsin was certainly greater; in fact, we have not been able to take account of the 400 ration texts relative to the reign of this king which are due to be published in OSP 3 by A.Westenholz (private communication).

111 These texts have been dealt with by R.B.Foster, USP, p.9-10; 54; 80-81, and TLAT, nos.13-32. The personal names of 38 scribes are mentioned in R.B.Foster, *Ethnicity and Onomastics in Sargonic Mesopotamia*, Or 51 (1982) p. 305-354.

112 For such an evaluation cf. H.Waetzoldt, *Gli scribi in Mesopotamia secondo le fonti neosumeriche*, Roma 1974, p.2.

113 Cf. P.Michalowski, *Charisma and Control: On Continuity and Change in Early Mesopotamian Systems*, in *The Organization of Power*, M.Gibson-R.D.Biggs (editors), SAOC 46 (1987), p.62-63.

hundred middle-to high-ranking scribes, like those of Fara, worked at the same time in the administration of the empire of Ur.

A comparison with the data given above seems to indicate that the scribes mentioned in the documentation of Fara may have had perhaps a far more wide-ranging jurisdiction than that of the simple administration of the city of Šuruppak. Certainly, however, the whole of the data given shows an administrative structure of whose size is unaspected for this period.

**C)** The administrative documentation relative to the last year of Fara and the analysis of it contained in Chapters I and II seems to demonstrate that a large number of men, at least 858 in **188** and 500 in **181**, probably together with the officials in charge of them, were transferred from the productive and organizational activity of the two principal administrative centres to recruitment for military purposes. The documentation we have studied so far seems to mention the number of men recruited; 6580 in the summary of **196**, of whom about 4,000 mentioned in **202** come from the other cities of Babylonia. This is the earliest testimony to a general mobilization of all able-bodied men fit for military service and war. It has also been noted that in the colophons of **182**, **189** and **192** there was an addition after the colophon stating that the men had received the rations of flour or barley due to them. In the colophons of **182**, **189**, **192**, **199**, and **200** clauses appear which indicate the need to provide sustenance for the men who have been recruited. The importance of the economic and logistical problems of having to provide for the sustenance of such a large number of men transpires from these data. This is shown by the need to have extremely large quantities of grain available like those mentioned in **38**, **40** and **41**. It is possible that the construction of a large number of silos near site XVII c,d, the only finds from the ED period (cf. Martin, *Fara*, p.47; G.Visicato, *Archéologie et documents écrits: les silos et les textes sur l'orge de Fara*, RA 87 (1993), pp.81-83), was dictated by the need to keep and to store grain for the sustenance of the enlisted men. Such an economic effort and such a mobilization involved not only Šuruppak but also the other cities of the Hexapolis in a war scenario which must have included the whole region. This suggests a threat of extraordinary proportions, something which had probably never happened before. We have found no element in the documentation to help us to understand who the enemy was the cities of the

Hexapolis and their allies had to face or what the reasons for the conflict were. The archaeological finds indicate that Šuruppak was destroyed by fire and practically disappeared as a leader from the Mesopotamian scene. The network of both economic and political relationships it had developed with the other cities of central and southern Babylonia which found concrete expression in the constitution of the Hexapolis and which had probably guaranteed, for a period we cannot delimit during ED II, conditions of controlled equilibrium of local conflicts dissolved with the destruction of Šuruppak. The organizational system of Šuruppak, as we have reconstructed it from the surviving documentation, could not have arisen in a short time given its complexity but must certainly have been the product of a development in Babylonia lasting several centuries. It is to be considered the earliest advanced structural organization of power which is attested in the documentation of Mesopotamia which is available to us and which we can comprehend [114] and one can suppose that only considerable difficulties could have brought about its downfall. From surface research (cf. Martin, *Fara*, p.14), it seems that during the Early Dynastic II period, the Euphrates underwent a modification of its course and as a consequence that branch which passed by Kiš, Nippur, Šuruppak and Uruk became a secondary channel while the branch which flowed through Adab, Umma and Lagaš became the principal one. This new situation, which clearly did not occur suddenly, must have brought about a slow but profound decline in the balanced conditions we have supposed. Šuruppak and its hinterland must have undergone a considerable reduction of its arable land and agricultural productivity which was necessary to maintain an organized bureaucratic apparatus like that which has gradually come to

---

114 We know nothing of Kiš except for some votive inscriptions of its kings and the mention of Mesalim in the cones of Entemena. The archaeological evidence seems to testify that during ED II and III there was a period of great splendour (cf.M.Gibson, T*he City and the area of Kis*, Miami 1972, pp.48, 58 and 268, Fig.27A). It seems certain that this city exercised a leadership role over Babylonia during this period and had developed a political and organizational system similar to that of Šuruppak. It cannot be excluded that the system current in Šuruppak had not derived from there. A group of about eighty tablets from the ED period was found in Kiš but unfortunately they have not yet been published. For a brief description of them cf. I.J.Gelb, *Ebla and Kish Civilization*, in L.Cagni (ed.), *La Lingua di Ebla*, Napoli 1981, p.55.

light, due to the decrease in the availability of water. But at the time to which our archives refer, the texts still testify to a notable prosperity when one considers both the total amount of the monthly rations to its subordinates, much greater than in later times (cf. *Šuruppak*, p.32-33), the large number of subordinates and finally the general availability of the enormous quantities of grain mentioned in the different documents. Even if at the time of our texts the phenomenon just mentioned must have been at an advanced stage, its effects do not seem to be perceptible from the documentation. The texts, particularly the barley texts of the II group but also the guruš texts, have demonstrated the existence of a sizeable river transport fleet and especially a large number of workers employed on ships (addir$_x$ and lú-má) with administrative centres which supervised this activity like the KISAL. This could indicate that the major source of wealth of Šuruppak might not have been agricultural production but commerce and river transport. In fact, it is possible that the fortunate position Šuruppak enjoyed during ED I and II enabled the city to develop this activity and consequently to control the flow of goods to and from the north. Using this as an interpretative key, the modification of the course of the river must have been an authentic catastrophe for the economy of the city because it caused the city to lose the control it had over the water transport routes. This situation accompanied by the rapid ascent of Ur, to whose wealth the royal tombs are witnesses, which, in all probability, controlled all the commerce in the Gulf zone (Dilmun, Magan and Meluhha) determined, for obvious reasons of survival, a situation of open conflict to which the texts examined in this study are a clear testimony. It cannot be affirmed that Ur was the adversary which destroyed Šuruppak since there is no textual support for such an affirmation but one cannot but observe that the period of the destruction of Šuruppak falls within the span of time from the the royal tombs of Ur to the reign of Mesannepada. In this lapse of time, Ur made a qualitative leap with respect to its previous agriculture-based economy (this latter is evidenced both by the archaic tablets and by archeological finds from the end of ED I, cf. H.T.Wright, *The Administration of Rural Production in an Early Mesopotamian Town*, Ann Arbor 1969, pp.25-42; 99-115). The finds from the royal tombs display a profusion of materials and objects coming from Iran, Afghanistan and especially from the countries of the Gulf; this seems to indicate that Ur had the monopoly of commerce in those areas (cf. H.Nissen, *Protostoria*, p.166 and M.Liverani, *Oriente*, p.182). If in a previous period this flow of goods probably passed through Šuruppak by river, then it must slowly have found other routes due to the variation in the course of the river. In addition, observing that Ur has no traces of destruction as a consequence of a conflict which seems to have involved the whole of Babylonia and that both during and after the fall of Šuruppak it continued to develop, it does not seem difficult to point to Ur as one of the cities which was advantaged by the disappearance of Šuruppak from the Babylonian political scene.

**D**) The characteristics of the society which the texts of Fara document can be summarized briefly as follows:

1) The administration of Šuruppak was strongly centralized and non-religious with a pyramidal structure at whose apex there seems to have been the sovereign, the énsi-GAR-gal. In its service was a large part of the active population as can be deduced from the number of persons enlisted and from the personnel in the employ of the various im-rus of the é-gal. The central administration seems to have possessed almost all the goods, in particular, all the arable land.
2) The structure of the society seems to have been stratified but not rigidly so, with the presence of various social levels which went from the guruš and the lú-ri-ri-ga employed in agricultural work and probably the personnel employed in weaving, to the artisans, the mid-ranking officials and finally, to the high-ranking officials.
3) Temple economic structures existed but they do not have the characteristics of self-sufficient households and they do not seem to own landed property. On the contrary, they seem to be totally part of the central administration and the officials who work within that structure seem to be its subordinates and to be maintained by it. Insofar as the texts testify, they seem to be almost exclusively employed in cattle breeding.
4) Private landed property existed as several land purchase contracts testify but this does not seem to influence the economic system in any way. In fact, the 25 or so purchase contracts which have survived concern small parcels of land whose extent, with rare exceptions, does not exceed on average 3 hectares (cf. ELTS, p.265-267).

5) Some economic and administrative structures like the é-gal-nimgir, some cattle breeding centres and probably also some of the im-rus of the é-gal and part of the transportation system perhaps operated at a regional level.

We believe that the socio-economic characteristics listed above as coming from one of the few settlements of the Early-Dynastic period with a large textual archive cannot be ignored in any attempt to reconstruct the evolutionary process of Babylonian society in the III millenium. Interesting models of this process have recently been proposed both by H.Nissen and P.Steinkeller (cf. H.Nissen, *Settlement Patterns and Material Culture of the Akkadian Period: Continuity and Discontinuity*, in *Akkad*, pp.91-106; P.Steinkeller, *Early Political Development in Mesopotamia*, in *Akkad*, pp.121-123).

# INDICES

# I Personal Names

# II Professional Names

a-a

1) $^{d}$sùd-anzu **187** v. III 1 3-4

a-zu$_5$

1) lú-é-zi **181** r. I 5-6; **182** r. I 2

ašgab

**188** r. II 7; **202** v. I 3

abgal

1) **188** r. III 1; **191** r. III 1'; **192** r. IV 5

2) lum-ma **195** r. II 5-6; mes-u$_4$-ba **195** r. IV 6

ad-KID

1) **202** v. I 6

2) é-nu-si **184** v. I 4-5; **182** r. IV 2-3

ad-NE

AK-$^{d}$sùd **213** r. II 1-2

addir$_x$

1) lú-má šà-addir$_x$-aka **209** v. III 2

agrig

1) dub-hul-tar **181** r. IV 2-3; NI.NI **181** r. IV 1; **185** r. II 2; šubur (?) **185** r. II 1

azlag$_4$

1) **192** r. IV 3

bahar$_4$

1) [é]-kur-ra **184** v. I 7-II 1

*bur-šu-ma*

1) šubur **195** r. III 2-3

dam-gàr

1) amar-šùba **195** r. III 3-4; GAR-ur-sag **195** r. VI 5-6

dub-sar sa$_{12}$-du$_5$

1) **193** r.I 3-4

dub-sar

1) a-hu-ti **183** r. III 2-3; **195** r. V 12-13; é-šùd-du$_{10}$ **187** v. I 4-5; é-zi-pa-è **212** r. I 6-II 1; lugal-á-mah **211** v. V' 2'-3'

dumu-dumu-šitim

1) **200** r. I 2

engar

1) ad-da **195** r. VII 4-5; amar-abzu **195** r. IV 10-11; é-na **195** r. IV 12-V 1; lugal-hé-gal **212** r. III 5-6; me-pa-è **195** r. VIII 9-10

(engar) é-géme

1) AN-nu-me **187** v. I 8-9

enku

1) **188** r. IV 5; **192** v. I 1; **193** r. II 6

2) [a]-nun-p[á] **195** v. I 1-2; uš-dù **195** r. VI 3-4

énsi-GAR

1) WF 126 r. I 2; 4; III 1; 3

2) sipa énsi-GAR **191** r. II 1

gal-nimgir

1) **188** r. III 2; NTSŠ 118 r. V 5; v. I 1; 5; II 5; IV 4; V 2

2) amar-$^{d}$gú-lá **187** v. I 9-II 1; AN-nu-me **195** r. IV 1-2; KA-lugal-da-zi **216** v. I 1'-2'

gala

1) AN-úr-šè NTSŠ 118 r. V 1-2; KA.Ú **212** r. I 1-2; nam-tur **212** r. I 3-4

galla$^{lá}$

1) NTSŠ 118 v. I 2

# III Geographical Names

## IV Terms Discussed

# Ugarit-Verlag Münster

Ricarda-Huch-Straße 6, D-48161 Münster

## *Abhandlungen zur Literatur Alt-Syrien-Palästinas und Mesopotamiens* (ALASP)

Herausgeber: *Manfried DIETRICH - Oswald LORETZ*

**Bd. 1** Manfried DIETRICH - Oswald LORETZ, *Die Keilalphabete.* 1988 (ISBN 3-927120-00-6), 376 S., DM 93,--; SFr 93,--; ÖS 650,--.

**Bd. 2** Josef TROPPER, *Der ugaritische Kausativstamm und die Kausativbildungen des Semitischen.* 1990 (ISBN 3-927120-06-5), 252 S., DM 71,--; SFr 71,--; ÖS 493,--.

**Bd. 3** Manfried DIETRICH - Oswald LORETZ, *Mantik in Ugarit.* Mit Beiträgen von Hilmar W. Duerbeck - Jan-Waalke Meyer - Waltraut C. Seitter. 1990 (ISBN 3-927120-05-7), 320 S., DM 98,--; SFr 98,--; ÖS 686,--.

**Bd. 5** Fred RENFROE, *Arabic-Ugaritic Lexical Studies.* 1992 (ISBN 3-927120-09-X). 212 S., DM 77,--; SFr 77,--; ÖS 535,--.

**Bd. 6** Josef TROPPER, *Die Inschriften von Zincirli.* 1993 (ISBN 3-927120-14-6). XII + 364 S., DM 108,--; SFr 108,--; ÖS 800,--.

**Bd. 7** *UGARIT - ein ostmediterranes Kulturzentrum im Alten Orient. Ergebnisse und Perspektiven der Forschung.* Vorträge gehalten während des Europäischen Kolloquiums am 11.-12. Februar 1993, hrsg. von Manfried DIETRICH und Oswald LORETZ. 1995 (ISBN 3-927120-17-0)(im Druck).

**Bd. 8** Manfried DIETRICH - Oswald LORETZ - Joaquín SANMARTÍN, *The Cuneiform Alphabetic Texts from Ugarit, Ras Ibn Hani and Other Places.* (*KTU: second, enlarged edition*). 1995 (ISBN 3-927120-24-3). XVI + 666 S., DM 120,--, SFr 120,--, ÖS 850,--.

**Bd. 9** Walter MAYER, *Politik und Kriegskunst der Assyrer.* 1995 (ISBN 3-927120-26-X). XVI + 545 S. DM 170,--; SFr 170,--; ÖS 1.190,--.

**Bd. 10** Giuseppe VISICATO, *The Bureaucracy of Šuruppak. Administrative Centres, Central Offices, Intermediate Structures and Hierarchies in the Economic Documentation of Fara.* 1995 (ISBN 3-927120-35-9)(im Druck)

**Bd. 11** Doris PRECHEL, *Die Göttin Išḫara. Ein Beitrag zur altorientalischen Religionsgeschichte.* 1996 (ISBN 3-927120-36-7)(im Druck)

## *Ugaritisch-Biblische Literatur* (UBL)

Herausgeber: *Oswald LORETZ*

**Bd. 4** Oswald LORETZ, *Regenritual und Jahwetag im Joelbuch.* 1986 (ISBN 3-88733-068-4), 189 S., DM 62,--; SFr 62,--; ÖS 430,--.

**Bd. 5** Oswald LORETZ - Ingo KOTTSIEPER, *Colometry in Ugaritic and Biblical Poetry. Introduction, Illustrations and Topical Bibliography.* 1987 (ISBN 3-88733-074-9), 166 pp., DM 52,--; SFr 52,--; ÖS 364,--.

**Bd. 6** Oswald LORETZ, *Die Königspsalmen.* Teil I. *Ps. 20; 21; 72; 101 und 144.* Mit einem Beitrag von Ingo Kottsieper zu *Papyrus Amherst.* 1988 (ISBN 3-927120-01-4), 261 S., DM 82,--; SFr 82,--; ÖS 574,--.

**Bd. 7** Oswald LORETZ, *Ugarit-Texte und Thronbesteigungspsalmen.* - Erweiterte Auflage von UBL 2. 1984-. 1988 (ISBN 3-927120-04-9), 550 S., DM 94,--; SFr 94,--; ÖS 650,--.

**Bd. 8** Marjo C.A. KORPEL, *A Rift in the Clouds.* 1990 (ISBN 3-927120-07-3), 736 S., DM 110,--; SFr 110,--; ÖS 770,--.

**Bd. 9** Manfried DIETRICH - Oswald LORETZ, *"Yahwe und seine Aschera". Anthropomorphes Kultbild in Mesopotamien, Ugarit, Israel - Das biblische Bilderverbot.* 1992 (ISBN 3-927120-08-1), 220 S., DM 76,--; SFr 76,--; ÖS 532,--.

**Bd. 10** Marvin H. POPE, *Probative Pontificating in Ugaritic and Biblical Literature. Collected Essays.* Ed. by Mark S. SMITH. 1994 (ISBN 3-927120-15-4), xvi + 406 S. DM 106,--; SFr 106,--; ÖS 760,--.

**Bd. 11** *Ugarit and the Bible. Proceedings of the International Symposium on Ugarit and the Bible, Manchester, September 1992.* Ed. by G.J. BROOKE, A.H.W. CURTIS, J.F. HEALEY. 1994 (ISBN 3-927120-22-7), X + 470 S., 3 Abb., DM 104,--; SFr 104,--; ÖS 750,--.

## *Altertumskunde des Vorderen Orients* (AVO)

Herausgeber: *Manfried DIETRICH - Reinhard DITTMANN - Oswald LORETZ*

Mitwirkende: *Nadja Cholidis - Maria Krafeld-Daugherty - Ellen Rehm*

**Bd. 1** Nadja CHOLIDIS, *Möbel in Ton - Untersuchungen zur archäologischen und religionsge-*

*schichtlichen Bedeutung der Terrakottamodelle von Tischen, Stühlen und Betten aus dem Alten Orient*. 1992 (ISBN 3-927120-10-3), XII + 323 S. + 46 Taf., DM 119,--; SFr 119,--; ÖS 833,--.

**Bd. 2** Ellen REHM, *Der Schmuck der Achämeniden*. 1992 (ISBN 3-927120-11-1), X + 358 S. + 107 Taf., DM 125,--; SFr 125,--; ÖS 875,--.

**Bd. 3** Maria KRAFELD-DAUGHERTY, *Wohnen im Alten Orient - Eine Untersuchung zur Verwendung von Räumen in altorientalischen Wohnhäusern*. 1994 (ISBN 3-927120-16-2), x + 404 S. + 41 Taf., DM 146,--; SFr 146,--; ÖS 1.030,--.

**Bd. 4** Manfried DIETRICH - Oswald LORETZ, Hrsg., *Festschrift für RUTH MAYER-OPIFICIUS mit Beiträgen von Freunden und Schülern*. 1994 (ISBN 3-927120-18-9), xviii + 356 S. + 256 Abb., DM 116,--; SFr 116,--; ÖS 835,--.

**Bd. 5** Gunnar LEHMANN, *Untersuchungen zur späten Einsenzeit in Syrien und Libanon. Stratigraphie und Keramikformen zwischen ca. 720 bis 300 v.Chr.* 1995 (ISBN 3-927120-33-2)(im Druck)

**Bd. 6** Ulrike LÖW, *Figürlich verzierte Metallgefäße aus Nord- und Nordwestiran - eine stilkritische Untersuchung*. 1996 (ISBN 3-927120-34-0)(im Druck)

## *Eikon*

Beiträge zur antiken Bildersprache
Herausgeber: *Klaus STÄHLER*

**Bd. 1** Klaus STÄHLER, *Griechische Geschichtsbilder klassischer Zeit*. 1992 (ISBN 3-927120-12-X), X + 120 S. + 8 Taf., DM 40,80; SFr 40,80; ÖS 285,--.

**Bd. 2** Klaus STÄHLER, *Form und Funktion. Kunstwerke als politsiches Ausdrucksmittel*. 1993 (ISBN 3-927120-13-8), VIII + 131 S. mit 54 Abb., DM 43,--; SFr 43,--; ÖS 348,--.

**Bd. 3** Klaus STÄHLER, *Zur Bedeutung des Formats*. 1994 (ISBN 3-927120-25-1)(im Druck).

## *Forschungen zur Anthropologie und Religionsgeschichte* (FARG)

Herausgeber: *Manfried DIETRICH - Oswald LORETZ*

**Bd. 27** Jehad ABOUD, *Die Rolle des Königs und seiner Familie nach den Texten von Ugarit*. 1994 (ISBN 3-927120-20-0), XI + 217 S., DM 38,50; SFr 38,50; ÖS 280,--.

**Bd. 28** Azad HAMOTO, *Der Affe in der altorientalischen Kunst*. 1995 (ISBN 3-927120-30-8), XII + 147 S. + 25 Tf./155 Abb.; DM 49,--; SFr 49,--; ÖS 350,--.

**Bd. 29** *Engel und Dämonen. Theologische, anthropologische und religionsgeschichtliche Aspekte des Guten und Bösen*. Vorträge gehalten während eines Symposiums zu Tartu/ Estland am 7.-8. April 1995, hsrg. von Gregor AHN - Manfried DIETRICH, 1995 (ISBN 3-927120-31-6) (im Druck)

## *Mitteilungen für Anthropologie und Religionsgeschichte* (MARG)

Herausgeber: *Gregor AHN - Manfried DIETRICH - Ansgar HÄUSSLING*

**Bd. 8** mit Beiträgen von M. DIETRICH, A. HÄUSSLING, Tschung-Sun KIM, T. KULMAR, O. LORETZ, K. MEISIG, A. RUPP†, S. STADNIKOW, H. VALK und Ü. VALK. 1994 (ISBN 3-927120-21-9), X + 219 S., DM 51,--; SFr 51,--; ÖS 370,--.

**Bd. 9** *In memoriam A. Rupp (1930 - 1993)* mit Beiträgen von G. AHN, Chong-Sok CHOE, M. DIETRICH, W. DUPRÉ, M. FRANZ, P. GERLITZ, A. HÄUSSLING, R.A.M. HÄUSSLING, K. KASEMAA, R. KÜHN, T. KULMAR, O. LORETZ, M. MANGOLD, W. MAYER, K. MEISIG, G. MULLER-BALLOT, W. SPRENGEL, S. STADNIKOW und Ü. VALK. 1994 (ISBN 3-927120-23-5), XXVI + 341 S. + 15 Taf., DM 62,--; SFr 62,--; ÖS 440,--.

**Bd. 10** mit Beiträgen von G. Ahn, M. Dietrich, P. Gerlitz, A. Häußling, V. Iwanow, T. Kulmar, R. Mayer-Opificius, M. Meisig und S. Stadnikow. 1995 (ISBN 3-927120-32-4), VI + 173 S., 31 Abb., DM 46,--; SFr 46,--; ÖS 322,--.

***Bei einem Abonnement der Reihen liegen die angegebenen Preise um ca. 15% tiefer.***

*Auslieferung durch -*
*Distributed by:*
**BDK Bücherdienst GmbH**
Kölner Straße 248
**D-51149 Köln**

*Distributor to North America:*
**Eisenbrauns, Inc.**
Publishers and Booksellers
POB 275
**Winona Lake, Ind. 46590**
U.S.A.